Introduction

This book is intended to help you prepare for the final examinations in IGCSE Mathematics, Extended Tier. This book covers all you need to know for the examination.

The topics have been arranged in groups: Number; Algebra; Shape and space; Statistics and probability. Each topic has been introduced in the same way: a reminder of definitions and techniques; one or more worked examples; a short exercise for each part. Finally, there is an examination question, together with a model answer, and then some examination questions for you to try. The answers to all the questions are at the back of the book. For full model answers to the exam questions, go to http://www.hoddermaths.co.uk. Throughout, there are explanations and tips to help you understand and make the most of your knowledge and understanding in answering questions in the actual examinations. Most of the topics are completed on two facing pages.

How to use this book

There are many ways of using the book. You could use it for reference when doing work from a different book. You could use it by opening a page randomly and checking that you can do the questions. The most satisfactory way, however, will be to use it systematically as part of your planned revision. Whether you choose to work through it in order or jump between topic areas, you can keep a check on your progress by using the Revision record at the front of the book.

Once you have chosen a topic, see if you can remember how to tackle the various parts. You can either work through the reminder sections and worked example first or try to answer the first question for yourself, to test if you can remember what it is about. Whichever way you do it, make sure you work through all the exercises and examination questions, as practice reinforces your learning. When you have completed a topic, don't forget to tick the box in the Revision record. If you know that your understanding is worse in certain topic areas, don't leave these to the end of your revision programme. Put them in at the start so that you will have time to return to them nearer the end of the revision period.

There are often many ways of tackling a problem. Not all of them will be in this book. If you have learned a different method that you understand, then keep on using it.

Examination tips

The examination papers will not tell you the formulae you need to use. You will have to learn and remember them. All those you need to know are clearly stated in the book. In some cases, you may have learned a formula in a different form. If so, continue to use it.

Make sure you read the instructions carefully, both those on the front of the paper and those in each question. Here are the meanings of some of the words used.

- **Write, write down, state** – little working out will be needed and no explanation is required.
- **Calculate, find** – something to be worked out, with a calculator if appropriate. It is a good idea to show the steps of your working as this may earn marks even if the answer is wrong.
- **Solve** – show all the steps in solving the equation.
- **Prove, show** – all the steps needed, including reasons, must be shown in a logical way.
- **Deduce, hence** – use a previous result to help you find the answer.
- **Draw** – draw as accurately and carefully as you can.
- **Sketch** – need not be accurate but should show the essential features.
- **Explain** – give (a) brief reason(s). The number of features you need to mention can be judged by looking at the marks. One mark probably means only one reason is required.

As well as this book, there are a lot of websites that will help you revise. Go to http://www.m-a.org.uk/links/index.htm for a list of links.

Brian Seager, 2004
Series editor

Revision Record/Contents

✓ **Tick the boxes to keep track of your progress**

Number

Integers (pages 2–3)
Multiples ☐
Factors ☐
Prime numbers; Prime factors ☐
Highest common factor (HCF) and lowest common multiple (LCM) ☐
Reciprocals ☐
Negative numbers ☐
Exam questions ☐

Powers and roots (pages 4–5)
Indices which are integers ☐
Exponential growth and decay ☐
Multiplying and dividing with indices ☐
Indices which are fractions ☐
Standard index form ☐
Exam questions ☐

Fractions and decimals (pages 6–7)
Adding and subtracting fractions ☐
Multiplying and dividing fractions ☐
Increasing or decreasing by a fraction ☐
Finding an amount before an increase or decrease ☐
Recurring and terminating decimals ☐
Changing a recurring decimal to a fraction ☐
Exam questions ☐

Percentages and ratios (pages 8–9)
Percentage increases or decreases ☐
Finding an amount before a percentage increase or decrease ☐
Ratios – simplest form; Using ratios ☐
Exam questions ☐

Mental methods (pages 10–11)
Important indices and rules ☐
Rounding to a given number of significant figures ☐
Standard index form ☐
Exam questions ☐

Written methods (pages 12–14)
Repeated proportional change and percentage change ☐
Direct proportion ☐
Inverse and other proportions ☐
Exam questions ☐

Calculator methods (pages 15–16)
Calculating with negative numbers ☐
Calculating with fractions ☐
Reciprocals ☐
Powers and roots ☐
Brackets ☐
Standard form ☐
Trigonometric keys ☐
Exam questions ☐

Solving problems (pages 17–18)
Some common money problems ☐
Compound measures ☐
Checking your work; Accuracy of answers ☐
Trial and improvement ☐
Exam questions ☐

Algebra

Symbols, indices, factors and expansions (pages 19–21)
Forming equations ☐
Multiplying brackets by single terms ☐
Multiplying two brackets ☐
Common factors ☐
Factorising by grouping ☐
Difference of two squares ☐
Indices ☐
Exam questions ☐

Linear equations (pages 22–23)
Solving equations ☐
Brackets in equations ☐
Dealing with the 'unknown' ☐
More than one set of brackets ☐
Fractions in equations ☐
Exam questions ☐

Formulae (pages 24–25)
Substituting in formulae ☐
Writing your own formulae ☐
Rearranging formulae ☐
Powers of the subject; Subject in twice ☐
Exam questions ☐

Direct and inverse proportion (pages 26–27)
Direct proportion ☐
Inverse proportion ☐
Exam questions ☐

Simultaneous equations and linear inequalities (pages 28–29)
Simultaneous equations ☐
Inequalities ☑
Exam questions ☐

Quadratic equations (pages 30–31)
Factorising quadratics ☐
Solving quadratic equations by factorising ☐
Solving quadratic equations that do not factorise ☐
Exam questions ☐

Algebraic fractions (page 32)
Simplifying fractions ☐
Solving equations with fractions ☐
Exam questions ☐

Sequences (pages 33–34)
Term-to-term rules ☐
Common sequences ☐
Position-to-term rules ☐
Other sequences ☐
Exam questions ☐

Graphs of linear functions (pages 35–36)
Gradient and y-intercept ☐
The general equation of a straight line $y = mx + c$ ☐
Parallel lines ☐
Exam questions ☐

Revision Record/Contents

Integers

Multiples

The multiples of a number are the numbers in its times table.

Now try these:

1 Find the first six multiples of the following.

(a) 4   (b) 9   (c) 15

Example

Find the multiples of 6 up to 30.

6, 12, 18, 24, 30

Factors

The factors of a number are the numbers which divide exactly into it.

Now try these:

2 Find the factors of the following.

(a) 24   (b) 40   (c) 32

Example

Find the factors of 36.

1×36 2×18 3×12 4×9 6×6

The factors of 36 are 1, 2, 3, 4, 6, 9, 12, 18 and 36.

It is easier to find factors by looking for pairs of numbers that multiply to give the number.

Prime numbers

Prime numbers are numbers which have only two factors; 1 and the number itself.

Example

Find the first five prime numbers.

2, 3, 5, 7, 11

Prime factors

Prime factors are factors which are also prime numbers.

Keep breaking the numbers into factors until you end up with prime numbers.

Now try these:

3 Write the following as a product of prime factors.

(a) 36   (b) 140   (c) 84

Example

Write 48 as a product of prime factors.

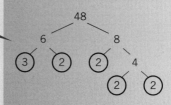

$48 = 2 \times 2 \times 2 \times 2 \times 3$ or $2^4 \times 3$

Highest common factor (HCF) and lowest common multiple (LCM)

- The HCF is the largest number that will divide into each of the given numbers.

Express each as a product of prime factors.

Choose the factors that are **common** to all three numbers.

Example

Find the HCF of 120, 36 and 84.

$120 = ②\times②\times 2 \times ③\times 5$
$36 = ②\times②\times 3 \times ③$
$84 = ②\times②\times③\times 7$
$HCF = 2 \times 2 \times 3 = 12$

- The LCM is the smallest number that can be divided exactly by each of the given numbers.

Express each as a product of prime factors.

Choose the largest number of primes.

Example

Find the LCM of 120, 36 and 84.

$120 = ② \times ② \times ② \times 3 \times ⑤$
$36 = 2 \times 2 \times ③ \times ③$
$84 = 2 \times 2 \times 3 \times ⑦$
$LCM = 2 \times 2 \times 2 \times 3 \times 3 \times 5 \times 7 = 2520$

Now try these:

4 Find the HCF and the LCM of the following.

   (a) 15 and 24   **(b)** 12 and 40   **(c)** 90, 54 and 36

Reciprocals

- The reciprocal of x is $\frac{1}{x}$.

- The reciprocal of $\frac{a}{b}$ is $\frac{b}{a}$.

Example

Find the reciprocals of:

(a) 4   **(b)** $\frac{2}{3}$ **(c)** 0·1

(a) $\frac{1}{4}$ **(b)** $\frac{3}{2}$ or 1·5   **(c)** $\frac{1}{0·1}$ or 10

Now try these:

5 Find the reciprocal of the following.

   (a) 5   **(b)** $\frac{1}{9}$ **(c)** $\frac{3}{4}$ **(d)** 0·2   **(e)** $2\frac{1}{2}$

Negative numbers

- When multiplying and dividing or when two signs follow each other then use the rules:

$$+ \; + \; = \; +$$
$$- \; - \; = \; +$$
$$- \; + \; = \; -$$
$$+ \; - \; = \; -$$

Example

Work out:

(a) $3 - (^-7)$ **(a)** $3 + 7 = 10$
(b) $^-4 \times 3$ **(b)** $^-12$
(c) $^-12 \div ^-6$ **(c)** $^+2$ or 2

- Combine the signs and numbers separately. A number with no sign is always +.

Now try these:

6 Work out the following.

   (a) $6 + (^-4)$ **(c)** $^-10 + (^-6)$ **(e)** $^-5 \times 3$ **(g)** $16 \div ^-4$
   (b) $^-4 - (^-3)$ **(d)** $9 - (^-2)$ **(f)** $^-20 \div ^-5$ **(h)** $^-8 \times ^-3$

Here is an exam question   ...and its solution

Write 30 as a product of prime factors.

$30 = 2 \times 3 \times 5$

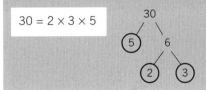

Now try these exam questions:

1 From the numbers from 10 up to 20, choose:
   (a) a multiple of 7
   (b) a factor of 36
   (c) a prime number.

2 Write 264 as a product of prime factors.

3 Find the HCF and LCM of 12 and 16.

4 Find the HCF and LCM of 10, 12 and 20.

5 Find the value of 4 multiplied by the reciprocal of 4. Show clear working to explain your answer.

6 Find the value of $(^-5)^2 + 4 \times ^-3$.

Powers and roots

Indices which are integers

Indices (or powers) give a short way of writing numbers multiplied by themselves.

> The 4 in 2^4 is called an index or power.

Now try these:

Find the value of the following.

1 3^4 3 3^{-2} 5 6^3

2 3^0 4 10^0 6 2^{-3}

Examples

$2^4 = 2 \times 2 \times 2 \times 2 = 16$
$2^3 = 2 \times 2 \times 2 \quad = 8$
$2^2 = 2 \times 2 \quad\quad = 4$
$2^1 = 2 \quad\quad\quad = 2$

Continuing the pattern:

$2^0 \quad = 1$
$2^{-1} = \frac{1}{2^1} = \frac{1}{2}$
$2^{-2} = \frac{1}{2^2} = \frac{1}{4}$

Don't forget that $n^0 = 1$ and $n^{-a} = \frac{1}{n^a}$ for any non-zero value of n.

Exponential growth and decay

- Use a constant multiplier – greater than 1 for growth, less than 1 for decay.

- Use the $\boxed{x^y}$ or $\boxed{\wedge}$ key.

Now try these:

7 Work out these.
   (a) $250 \times (1 \cdot 03)^{10}$
   (b) $(0 \cdot 89)^{15}$
   (c) Stanley put \$500 in a bank account. The interest was 4% per annum, compound. How much was in the account after seven years?
   (d) A radioactive substance loses 5% of its mass every hour. What proportion remains after 24 hours?

Example

(a) A car depreciates by 30% every year. It cost \$9000 new. How much is it worth after five years?
(b) A population of bacteria increases by 6% every hour. By what factor has the population grown after 24 hours?

(a) $9000 \times (0 \cdot 7)^5$

$\boxed{9}\boxed{0}\boxed{0}\boxed{0}\boxed{\times}\boxed{0}\boxed{\cdot}\boxed{7}\boxed{x^y}\boxed{5}\boxed{=}$ \$1512

(b) $(1 \cdot 06)^{24}$

$\boxed{1}\boxed{\cdot}\boxed{0}\boxed{6}\boxed{\wedge}\boxed{2}\boxed{4}\boxed{=}$ 4.0489...

The population has grown approximately four times.

Multiplying and dividing with indices

- Multiplying.
  $n^a \times n^b = n^{a+b}$

> Add the powers.

- Dividing.
  $n^a \div n^b$ or $\frac{n^a}{n^b} = n^{a-b}$

> Subtract the powers.

- Powers of powers.
  $(n^a)^b = n^{ab}$

> Multiply the powers.

Now try these:

Simplify the following.

8 $5^2 \times 5^8$ 10 $4a^6 \times 2a^3$ 12 $(c^2)^5$

9 $6^5 \div 6^2$ 11 $\dfrac{12a^5b^2}{2a^3b^3}$ 13 $(2x^4)^3$

Examples

$3^2 \times 3^4 = 3^6$ > $2 + 4 = 6$
$2y^4 \times 3y^5 = 6y^9$ > $4 + 5 = 9$

Example

$3^5 \div 3^3 = 3^2$ > $5 - 3 = 2$

Example

$(2^3)^4 = 2^{12}$ > $3 \times 4 = 12$

For adding and subtracting, indices are not so helpful. There is no shortcut rule.

Example $3^2 + 3^3 = 9 + 27 = 36$

See page 21 for more algebra practice with indices.

Indices which are fractions

- Using the laws of indices, $n^{\frac{1}{2}} \times n^{\frac{1}{2}} = n^{\frac{1}{2}+\frac{1}{2}} = n^1 = n$ therefore $n^{\frac{1}{2}} = \sqrt{n}$.

- Similarly we can show that
  $n^{\frac{1}{a}} = \sqrt[a]{n}$ and $n^{\frac{a}{b}} = \sqrt[b]{n^a}$ or $(\sqrt[b]{n})^a$.

Examples

$64^{\frac{1}{3}} = \sqrt[3]{64} = 4$

$125^{-\frac{2}{3}} = \dfrac{1}{(\sqrt[3]{125})^2} = \dfrac{1}{5^2} = \dfrac{1}{25}$ or $0 \cdot 4$

Now try these:

Write down the value of these.

14 $36^{\frac{1}{2}}$ **15** $1000^{-\frac{1}{3}}$

Use your calculator to find the following.

16 $90^{\frac{2}{3}}$, correct to 1 d.p. **17** $1024^{-\frac{2}{5}}$

Page 10 gives more practice with indices

The examples show non-calculator methods. Also try to obtain the answers using the power keys on your calculator.

Know how to use the root and power buttons on your calculator.

Standard index form

- This is used for large or very small numbers.
- They are written in the form $a \times 10^n$, where n is an integer and $1 \leqslant a < 10$.
- To multiply or divide numbers in standard form without a calculator, use the rules of indices.

$$(3 \times 10^6) \times (5 \times 10^8) = 15 \times 10^{8+6} = 15 \times 10^{14}$$
$$= 1.5 \times 10^{15}$$

Examples
$3\,500\,000 = 3.5 \times 10^6$ $0.000\,42 = 4.2 \times 10^{-4}$

Don't forget – to enter standard form on a scientific calculator, use the [EXP] key, not [×][1][0]

Example to enter 3.5×10^6, press [3][.][5][EXP][6].

Many calculators display numbers in standard form as if they were powers. You need to interpret your calculator display and write down the number correctly in standard form.

Now try these:

Write the following as ordinary numbers.

18 3.72×10^5 **19** 4.8×10^{-4}

Write the following in standard form.

20 $0.000\,058\,3$ **21** $75\,600\,000$

Work out, first without a calculator then with one.

22 $(8 \times 10^5) \times (1.5 \times 10^8)$ **23** $(5 \times 10^7) \div (2 \times 10^{-3})$

Here is an exam question   ...and its solution

This question tests the rules of indices and standard form without a calculator.

(a) Simplify.

(i) $\dfrac{pq^3 \times p^2}{p^5 q}$ **(ii)** $\left(p^8\right)^{-\frac{3}{4}}$

(b) Write in standard form.
(i) $41\,000\,000$ **(ii)** $0.000\,062\,9$

(c) Calculate, giving your answer in standard form.

(i) $(3 \times 10^{-9}) \times (7 \times 10^{11})$ **(ii)** $\dfrac{6 \times 10^4}{2 \times 10^{-4}}$

(a) (i) $p^{-2} q^2$ or $\dfrac{q^2}{p^2}$

(ii) p^{-6} or $\dfrac{1}{p^6}$

for p: $1 + 2 - 5 = {}^-2$
for q: $3 - 1 = 2$
$8 \times \dfrac{{}^-3}{4} = {}^-6$

(b) (i) 4.1×10^7
(ii) 6.29×10^{-5}

(c) (i) 21×10^2
$= 2.1 \times 10^3$
(ii) 3×10^8

$7 \times 3 = 21$, ${}^-9 + 11 = 2$
$21 = 2.1 \times 10^1$
$6 \div 2 = 3$, $4 - {}^-4 = 8$

Now try these exam questions:

1 Write the following as whole numbers or fractions.
(a) 9^{-2} **(b)** 9^0 **(c)** $27^{\frac{1}{3}}$

2 (a) Write the following as whole numbers or fractions.
(i) 4^0 **(ii)** $9^{\frac{1}{2}}$

(b) Evaluate $(3 \times 10^{-2}) \times (8 \times 10^5)$, giving your answer in standard form.

3 (a) Work out the exact value of $2^{-3} \times 16^{\frac{1}{2}}$.

(b) Simplify as far as possible $\sqrt{p^4 q^{-3}} \times \sqrt{\dfrac{q}{p^{-2}}}$.

4 (a) Simplify as far as possible $\dfrac{12p^2q}{3p} \times 2q^2$.

(b) Work out, as a fraction, the exact value of $\left(\dfrac{49}{4}\right)^{-\frac{3}{2}}$.

5 (a) Work out $(3.0 \times 10^4) \times (6.0 \times 10^3)$, writing the answer in standard form.

(b) A terawatt is 10^{12} watts. A power station produces 1.2×10^8 watts. Write this in terawatts.

6 Calculate the difference between 5^{-2} and 2^{-5}. Give your answer in standard form.

7 A block of ice is melting. Its volume reduces by 15% each hour.

It starts as 80 litres. What is its volume after 6 hours?

Fractions and decimals

Adding and subtracting fractions

- Change the fractions to the same denominator then add or subtract the numerators.
- When mixed numbers are involved, deal with the whole numbers first.
- In subtraction, when the first fraction part is smaller than the second, you can change a whole number to a fraction.

Example

$2 \times 8 = 16$

$$2\frac{2}{3} + 1\frac{3}{8} = 3 + \frac{2}{3} + \frac{3}{8}$$

$3 \times 3 = 9$

$$= 3 + \frac{16}{24} + \frac{9}{24} = 3\frac{25}{24} = 4\frac{1}{24}$$

Example

$3 \times 8 = 24$

$$3\frac{1}{4} - 1\frac{2}{5} = 2 + \frac{1}{4} - \frac{2}{5}$$

$$= 2 + \frac{5}{20} - \frac{8}{20} = 1 + \frac{20}{20} + \frac{5}{20} - \frac{8}{20} = 1\frac{17}{20}$$

Change 1 to $\frac{20}{20}$.

Now try these:

$1 \quad 2\frac{3}{8} + 3\frac{1}{6}$ $3 \quad 3\frac{4}{5} - 2\frac{1}{4}$ $5 \quad 4\frac{2}{5} - 1\frac{5}{6}$

$2 \quad 1\frac{2}{3} + 3\frac{4}{5}$ $4 \quad 3\frac{3}{4} - 2\frac{2}{3}$ $6 \quad \frac{3}{8} + \frac{3}{4} - \frac{1}{6}$

$1 = \frac{2}{2} = \frac{3}{3}$ etc.

Multiplying and dividing fractions

- When mixed numbers are involved, first change to top-heavy fractions.
- To multiply fractions, multiply the numerators and the denominators and then simplify.
- To divide fractions, invert the second fraction and multiply.

Example

$$2\frac{1}{2} \times 1\frac{2}{5} = \frac{5}{2} \times \frac{7}{5}$$

Make fractions top-heavy.

$$= \frac{1}{2} \times \frac{7}{1}$$

Cancel by 5.

$$= \frac{7}{2} = 3\frac{1}{2}$$

Example

$$3\frac{3}{4} \div \frac{1}{2}$$

Make fraction top-heavy.

$$= \frac{15}{4} \div \frac{1}{2}$$

Invert the second fraction and multiply.

$$= \frac{15}{4} \times \frac{2}{1}$$

$$= \frac{15}{2} \times \frac{1}{1}$$

Cancel by 2.

$$= \frac{15}{2} = 7\frac{1}{2}$$

Now try these:

$7 \quad 2\frac{1}{3} \times 4\frac{1}{2}$ $9 \quad 2\frac{2}{5} \times 4\frac{3}{4}$ $11 \quad 3\frac{1}{3} \div \frac{1}{2}$

$8 \quad 3\frac{1}{3} \times 1\frac{1}{5}$ $10 \quad 2 \div \frac{3}{5}$ $12 \quad 4\frac{1}{5} \div 2\frac{1}{3}$

Increasing or decreasing by a fraction

To increase or decrease an amount by a fraction:

- add or subtract the fraction to or from 1
- multiply by the new fraction.

Example

Increase 18 by $\frac{1}{3}$.

$$18 \times \frac{4}{3} = 24$$

$1 + \frac{1}{3} = \frac{4}{3}$

Finding an amount before an increase or decrease

To find the amount before an increase or decrease:

- add or subtract the fraction to or from 1
- divide by the fraction.

Old price = New price $\div \left(1 + \frac{1}{5}\right)$

Example

After an increase of $\frac{1}{5}$, the cost of a coat is $54. What was it before the increase?

Old price = $54 \div 1\frac{1}{5}$ = $54 \div \frac{6}{5}$ = $54 \times \frac{5}{6}$ = $45

Now try these:

13 Increase 20 by $\frac{1}{4}$.

14 Decrease 15 by $\frac{2}{5}$.

In questions 15 to 18 find the amounts before the increase or decrease.

15 New amount = \$35. Increase: $\frac{1}{4}$.

17 New amount = \$278·20. Increase: $\frac{3}{10}$.

16 New amount = \$171. Decrease: $\frac{1}{10}$.

18 New amount = \$1071. Decrease: $\frac{2}{5}$.

Recurring and terminating decimals

- All fractions are equal to either recurring or terminating decimals.
- The fractions equal to terminating decimals have denominators whose only prime factors are 2 and/or 5.

Example

Write these fractions as decimals.

(a) $\frac{1}{8}$ (b) $\frac{1}{6}$ (c) $\frac{13}{20}$ (d) $\frac{7}{25}$ (e) $\frac{3}{7}$

(a) 0·125 — Terminating, prime factor 2.
(b) 0·1$\dot{6}$ — Recurring, prime factors 2 and 3.
(c) 0·65 — Terminating, prime factors 2 and 5.
(d) 0·28 — Terminating, prime factor 5.
(e) 0·$\dot{4}$2857$\dot{1}$ — Recurring, prime factor 7.

Changing a recurring decimal to a fraction

The method for doing this is best illustrated by an example.

Multiply by 10^n where n is the number of recurring figures.

Now try these:

Express these decimals as fractions in their lowest terms.

19 0·$\dot{7}$ **20** 0·$\dot{6}\dot{1}$ **21** 0·4$\dot{1}\dot{6}$

Example

Express 0·$\dot{4}\dot{2}$ as a fraction in its lowest terms.

Let $r = 0\cdot\dot{4}\dot{2} = 0\cdot42424242...$
$100r = 42\cdot424242$ — Multiply by 100.
Subtract: $99r = 42$
$r = \frac{42}{99} = \frac{14}{33}$

Here is an exam question   ...and its solution

A railway has a special offer on some fares. This is the advertisement:

What is the cost of the normal fare?

Fares Reduced
$\frac{1}{3}$ off normal fare
You pay only \$75.

Fare is reduced by $\frac{1}{3}$.

To find normal fare divide by $\left(1 - \frac{1}{3}\right)$.

\$112·50 Normal fare is $\$75 \div \frac{2}{3} = 75 \times \frac{3}{2}$

Now try these exam questions:

1 Work out, writing the answers as fractions.
(a) $2\frac{3}{4} + \frac{3}{8}$ (b) $3\frac{2}{3} - 2\frac{1}{2}$

2 Work out the following. Give your answers as fractions as simply as possible.
(a) $1\frac{3}{5} \times 2\frac{2}{9}$ (b) $1\frac{1}{4} + 2\frac{3}{5}$

3 All the prices in Helen's shop are reduced by $\frac{1}{5}$ in a sale.
(a) What is the sale price of a jumper that cost \$27·50 before the sale?
(b) The sale price of a dress is \$72. What was the price of the dress before the sale?

4 Work out, giving your answers as fractions in their lowest terms.
(a) $2\frac{3}{8} - 1\frac{1}{2}$ (b) $2\frac{1}{4} \div 1\frac{4}{5}$

5 $h = \frac{2xy}{x+y}$ Find h when $x = \frac{2}{5}$, $y = \frac{2}{7}$.

6 (a) Express 0·$\dot{1}\dot{4}$ as a fraction in its lowest terms.
(b) Without working them out, state whether these fractions are equal to terminating or recurring decimals. Explain your answers.
(i) $\frac{4}{7}$ (ii) $\frac{3}{40}$ (iii) $\frac{5}{6}$ (iv) $\frac{4}{9}$

7 In an election $\frac{3}{4}$ of the voters chose the Orange party. The number who chose the Orange party was 13 845. How many people voted altogether?

Percentages and ratios

Percentage increases or decreases

To find a percentage increase or decrease:
- add or subtract the percentage from 100
- change to a decimal
- multiply.

> If an amount increases by 5% each year, multiply by $(1 \cdot 05)^n$ to find the amount after n years.

> If an amount decreases by 5% each year, multiply by $(0 \cdot 95)^n$ to find the amount after n years.

Example

$3500 is increased by 2% per year.
(a) What is the amount after one year?
(b) What is the amount after five years? Give the answer to the nearest cent.

(a) $100 + 2 = 102\% = 1 \cdot 02$ *Multiply by 1·02.*
After one year $= 3500 \times 1 \cdot 02 = \$3570$
(b) After five years $= 3500 \times (1 \cdot 02)^5$
$= \$3864 \cdot 2828 = \$3864 \cdot 28$

Now try these:

1 Increase:
   (a) $84 by 7%
   (b) $6300 by 2·5%

2 Decrease:
   (a) $12 by 10%
   (b) $5900 by 3%

3 Find the value of $2000 when it is decreased by 5% each year for three years.

4 The insurance value of a house increased by 6% each year. In 1999 it was valued at $152 000. What was its insurance value four years later?

Finding an amount before a percentage increase or decrease

To find the original amount before a percentage increase:
- add the percentage to 100
- change to a decimal
- divide.

If it is a decrease, subtract instead of adding.

Example

The price of a skirt was reduced by 5%. It now costs $27·55. What was the original price?

Decrease, so new price $= 100 - 5 = 95\%$ of original price.

> To find original price divide by 0·95 (95% = 0·95).

Original price $= 27 \cdot 55 \div 0 \cdot 95 = \$29.$

Now try these:

5 A quantity is increased by 3%. It is now 61·8. What was it before the increase?

6 A wage is increased by 6% and is now $8692. What was it before the increase?

7 An amount is decreased by 2·5% and is now $1170. What was the amount before the decrease?

8 A garage decreased the price of all its cars by 7·5%. A car is now priced at $7511. What was the price before the discount?

Ratios – simplest form

- To write a ratio in its simplest form change the parts to the same units and cancel by any common factor.
- To write as $1 : n$, divide the second part by the first.

Example

Write these ratios
(a) in their simplest form
(b) as $1 : n$.
(i) $4 : 14$ (ii) 75 cents : $4 (iii) 5 cm : 4 km.

Cancel by 2.

Change to centimetres and cancel by 5.

Change to cents and cancel by 25.

(a) (i) $2 : 7$
(ii) $75 : 400 = 3 : 16$
(iii) $5 : 400 000 = 1 : 80 000$
(b) (i) $1 : 3 \cdot 5$ (ii) $1 : 5 \cdot 33$ (iii) $1 : 80 000$

Divide by 2. *Divide by 3.*

Now try these:

9 Write these ratios
   (a) in their simplest form
   (b) as $1 : n$.
   (i) $4 : 12$
   (ii) $24 : 9$
   (iii) 400 m : 2 km
   (iv) 80 cents : 2 dollars

Using ratios

To share a total amount in a given ratio, first add the parts of the ratio together. Find the multiplier by dividing the total amount by the sum of the ratio parts. Then use the same multiplier for the parts.

Example

$150 is shared in the ratio 3 : 4 : 5. How much is each part?

Total of ratios 12. Multiplier is 150 ÷ 12.

Parts are $3 \times 150 \div 12 = \$37.50$
$4 \times 150 \div 12 = \$50$
$5 \times 150 \div 12 = \$62.50$

> Multiply each part by 150 ÷ 12.

Now try these:

10 Share $18 in the ratio 4 : 5.

11 To make pink paint, red and white are mixed in the ratio 2 : 5. How much pink paint can be made if six litres of red are used?

12 Share $177 in the ratio 1 : 2 : 3.

Here is an exam question ...and its solution

(a) Jenny used to go to the village hairdresser where a trim cost $4. The hairdresser left so she went to a salon in town. A trim there cost $30. What percentage increase is this?

(b) At the town salon the prices have gone up several times. The last increase was 6%. She now pays $37·10. How much did she pay before the last increase?

(a) 650%   Increase = $26. Original was $4.
Percentage increase $= \frac{26}{4} \times 100$

(b) $35   New = 106% of previous. (1·06)

> Previous is wanted so divide by 1·06.

Previous = 37·10 ÷ 1·06

Now try these exam questions:

1 My computer cost $899. It falls in value by 30% each year.
   (a) What is its value after one year?
   (b) Show that, after four years, it is worth less than a quarter of its original cost.

2 All clothes in a sale were reduced by 15%. Mark bought a coat for $68 in the sale. How much did it cost before the sale?

3 Catherine bought a flat for $84 000. The value of the flat increased by 8% each year. Calculate the value of the flat, correct to the nearest hundred pounds, at the end of six years.

4 In 1997 a store added VAT at 17·5% to the basic price of furniture.
   (a) A sofa had a basic price of $650. What was its selling price inclusive of VAT?
   (b) During a sale the store said 'We pay the VAT!' What percentage discount on the normal selling price was the store giving?

5 Eau de Parfum is made from three parts flower extract, eight parts water and nine parts alcohol.
   (a) How much water does a 250 ml bottle of Eau de Parfum contain?
   (b) How many litres of Eau de Parfum can be made with 45 litres of flower extract?

6 To make a map, a scale of 5 cm : 2 km was used.
   (a) Aberville and Banchester are 7 km apart. How far are they apart on the map?
   (b) Write the ratio 5 cm : 2 km as simply as possible.

7 (a) In a survey of 4000 adults, 2800 said they were in favour of carrying organ donor cards. Work out the percentage who said they were in favour.
   (b) In another survey 300 people said they did carry donor cards. The ratio of men to women carrying donor cards was 7 : 8. Work out the number of men and the number of woman carrying donor cards.

Mental methods

Important indices and rules

You need to know the following facts:

$$a^0 = 1, \quad a^{-1} = \frac{1}{a}, \quad a^{-2} = \frac{1}{a^2},$$

$$a^{-4} = \frac{1}{a^4}, \quad a^{\frac{1}{2}} = \sqrt{a}, \quad a^{\frac{1}{3}} = \sqrt[3]{a}.$$

Now try these:

1 Write down the values of the following.

(a) $16^{\frac{1}{2}} \times 27^{\frac{1}{3}}$ (d) $3^{-2} \times 9^0$

(b) $25^{\frac{1}{2}} \div 100^{\frac{1}{2}}$ (e) $81^{\frac{1}{2}} \times 3^{-2}$

(c) 6^{-2}

2 Write these numbers in ascending order.

$4^{\frac{1}{2}} \quad 4^{-2} \quad 4^0 \quad 4^{\frac{1}{3}} \quad 4^2$

Example

Write down the answers to the following.

(a) 3^0 (c) 4^{-2} (e) $125^{\frac{1}{3}}$

(b) 9^{-1} (d) $64^{\frac{1}{2}}$

(a) 1   (c) $\frac{1}{4^2} = \frac{1}{16}$ (e) $\sqrt[3]{125} = 5$

(b) $\frac{1}{9}$ (d) $\sqrt{64} = 8$

Rounding to a given number of significant figures

Significant figures are counted from the left.

Start with the first non-zero figure.

Remember, when rounding, that zeros are kept to show the size of the number.

If the value of the first digit being ignored is 5 or more, round up.

Now try these:

3 Write the following numbers correct to 2 s.f.

(a) 5·384   (c) 0·3142

(b) 12·049   (d) 45 300

4 Write the following numbers correct to 1 s.f.

(a) 23·99   (c) 0·695

(b) 123·99   (d) 1·345

Example

Write the following numbers correct to 3 s.f.

(a) 3·6583   (c) 95 770

(b) 0·5432   (d) 0·050 43

Count all the non-zero digits from the left.

(a) 3·66   (c) 95 800

(b) 0·543   (d) 0·0504

Standard index form

- Standard index form, or standard form, is used to write a large or small number as a number between 1 and 10 multiplied by a power of 10.

This is sometimes expressed as

$a \times 10^n$, where $0 < a < 10$

and n is an integer (positive or negative).

Example

Write these numbers in standard index form.

(a) 16 000   (a) $1·6 \times 10^4$

(b) 432   (b) $4·32 \times 10^2$

(c) 0·314   (c) $3·14 \times 10^{-1}$

(d) 54 320 000   (d) $5·432 \times 10^7$

Example

Write these numbers out in full.

(a) 4×10^3 (a) 4 000

(b) $2·74 \times 10^4$ (b) 27 400

(c) $5·3 \times 10^{-1}$ (c) 0·53

(d) $4·68 \times 10^{-4}$ (d) 0·000 468

- Some other rules of indices which will apply when working in standard form:

$a^x \times a^y = a^{x+y}$,

$a^x \div a^y = a^{x-y}$.

Now try these:

5 Write these numbers in standard index form.
   (a) 46 000   **(c)** 3 600 000
   (b) 0·0484   **(d)** 5965

6 Write these numbers out in full.
   (a) 8×10^6 **(c)** $7 \cdot 7 \times 10^1$
   (b) $9 \cdot 4 \times 10^3$ **(d)** $3 \cdot 03 \times 10^{-4}$

7 Evaluate $\dfrac{7 \cdot 5 \times 10^{-4}}{2 \cdot 5 \times 10^9}$. Give your answer in standard form.

8 Evaluate $(3 \times 10^{-3}) \times (8 \times 10^7)$. Give your answer in standard form.

9 Work out $(4 \times 10^5) \div (8 \times 10^{-6})$. Give your answer in standard index form.

10 Find the approximate value of $\dfrac{(8 \cdot 42 \times 10^8) \times (2 \cdot 83 \times 10^{-4})}{6 \cdot 074 \times 10^5}$ by writing all the numbers correct to 1 s.f.

Here is an exam question   ...and its solution

The Astronomical Unit is used to measure large distances between stars.

One Astronomical Unit is $1 \cdot 496 \times 10^{11}$ m.

(a) What are 100 Astronomical Units? Give your answer in standard form.

(b) Light travels at $2 \cdot 998 \times 10^8$ m/s. Write this as an ordinary number.

(a) $1 \cdot 496 \times 10^{13}$ m

100 AU
$= 1 \cdot 496 \times 10^{11} \times 10^2$

(b) 299 800 000 m/s

$2 \cdot 998 \times 10^8$
$= 2 \cdot 998 \times 100 000 000$

Now try these exam questions:

1 Estimate the value of $\dfrac{196 \cdot 8 - 48 \cdot 3}{\sqrt{0 \cdot 044}}$.

2 Evaluate $\dfrac{2^8 \times 2}{2^{-2}}$,
   (a) expressing your answer in the form 2^n
   (b) expressing your answer in standard form correct to 3 s.f.

3 A radar transmitter sends out a beam of radio waves at a frequency of 24 thousand million pulses per second. Write this figure in standard form.

4 Estimate the value of $\left(50^{\frac{1}{2}} + 80^{\frac{1}{2}}\right) \times \left(10^{\frac{1}{2}} + 25^{\frac{1}{2}}\right)$.

5 The orbit of Halley's Comet means that it passes the Earth every 76 years. At its furthest point it is 35 Astronomical Units from Earth. An Astronomical Unit is $1 \cdot 496 \times 10^{11}$ m.

   What is its maximum distance from Earth? Give your answer in standard form, in metres.

Written methods

Repeated proportional change

- To increase a quantity by say $\frac{1}{5}$, one way is to multiply by $\frac{1}{5}$ and add the result on to the original. A quicker way is to multiply by $1 + \frac{1}{5} = \frac{6}{5}$ or $1 \cdot 2$.

- If this is repeated then it is equivalent to multiplying by $\left(\frac{6}{5}\right)^2$ or $1 \cdot 2^2$. So to increase a quantity by $\frac{1}{5}$ four times you multiply by $\left(\frac{6}{5}\right)^4$ or $1 \cdot 2^4$.

- Similarly, to reduce a quantity by $\frac{1}{12}$ you multiply by $1 - \frac{1}{12} = \frac{11}{12}$. So to reduce a quantity by $\frac{1}{12}$ three times you multiply by $\left(\frac{11}{12}\right)^3$. In this case since $\frac{11}{12}$ is a recurring decimal it is better to use fractions.

Remember the power button on your calculator is $\boxed{y^x}$ or $\boxed{x^y}$ or $\boxed{\wedge}$.

Example

A company promised to increase the value of an investment by $\frac{1}{12}$ every year. If this promise is kept how much would an investment of $500 be worth in five years?

$500 \times \left(\frac{13}{12}\right)^5 = \$746 \cdot 07.$

Example

In a town's road safety campaign the aim is to reduce accidents by $\frac{1}{10}$ every year. If there were 400 accidents in 2000, and the campaign is successful, how many should there be in 2004?

$400 \times \left(\frac{9}{10}\right)^4 = 262$

Repeated percentage change

This is done in a similar way.

- To increase by say 6% for five years you multiply by $1 \cdot 06^5$.

- To decrease by 15% four times in succession you multiply by $0 \cdot 85^4$.

Example

Sheila invests $600 at 4% compound interest. How much will the investment be worth after ten years?

$600 \times 1 \cdot 04^{10} = \$888 \cdot 15$

Example

A car depreciates in value by 12% per year. If it cost $12 500 when new, how much will it be worth after five years?

$12\,500 \times 0 \cdot 88^5 = \$6596 \cdot 65$

Now try these:

1 What do you multiply by to increase by:
  (a) $\frac{1}{7}$ (b) $\frac{3}{8}$ (c) 7% (d) 32% (e) $17\frac{1}{2}$%?

2 What do you multiply by to decrease by:
  (a) $\frac{1}{7}$ (b) $\frac{3}{8}$ (c) 7% (d) 32% (e) $17\frac{1}{2}$%?

3 The volume of a block of ice reduces by $\frac{1}{5}$ every hour. If the original volume was 350 cm^3, what will the volume be after three hours?

4 A headline reads 'Violent crimes going up by $\frac{1}{10}$ every year.' If there were 18 000 violent crimes in 1995, how many does this suggest there were in 2001?

5 Gina invests $2000 at 3% compound interest. What will this be worth
  (a) after three years (b) after ten years?

6 A car's value depreciates by 13% per year. If it cost $9990 when new in 1998, what will it be worth in 2004?

7 An antique increases in value by 60% every five years. If it was worth $300 in 1980, what will it be worth in 2005?

8 The number of a certain species of bird has been decreasing by $\frac{1}{20}$ every year. If there were 20 000 in 1990, how many were there in 2000?

Direct proportion

- If quantities vary in direct proportion it means that:
  if you double one quantity, you double the other;
  if you treble one quantity, you treble the other;
  if you halve one quantity, you halve the other; and so on.

- If x and y vary in direct proportion the graph of y against x will be a straight line passing through the origin.

In this case the equation will be in the form $y = kx$.

Now try these:

9 The time taken to mark students' homework is directly proportional to the number of students.
If it takes two hours to mark 16 students' homework, how long does it take to mark
(a) 4 (b) 32 (c) 40 students' homework?

Example

The total cost of books is directly proportional to the number of books bought. If 30 books cost \$240, how much will (a) 120 books (b) 15 books cost?

(a) $120 = 4 \times 30$
so 120 books cost $4 \times \$8 = \$960$
(b) $15 = \frac{1}{2} \times 30$
so 15 books cost $\frac{1}{2} \times \$240 = \$120$
Alternatively you can work out the cost of 1 book = $240 \div 30 = \$8$ first and then multiply by the number of books.
So $C = 8n$ is the equation connecting the number of books (n) and the total cost in pounds (C).

Inverse and other proportions

- Inverse proportion means that: if one quantity is doubled, the other is halved; if one quantity is multiplied by three, the other is divided by three; and so on.
  So $y \propto \frac{1}{x}$ and the equation is
  $y = k \times \frac{1}{x}$ or $y = \frac{k}{x}$.

- Other proportions are dealt with in the same way:
  if y is proportional to x^2 then $y \propto x^2$ or $y = kx^2$;
  if y is inversely proportional to x^2, then $y \propto \frac{1}{x^2}$ and
  $y = k \times \frac{1}{x^2}$ or $y = \frac{k}{x^2}$.

Now try these:

10 The time (t hours) taken to build a wall is inversely proportional to the number of builders (b).
Ten builders can build the wall in four hours.
(a) Find an equation connecting b and t.
(b) How long would 12 builders take?
(c) Find the number of builders needed to build the wall in eight hours.

11 The mass of a sphere (m g) is proportional to the cube of the radius (r cm). A sphere of radius 20 cm has a mass of 24 000 g.
(a) Find an equation connecting m and r.
(b) Find the mass of a sphere of radius 5 cm.
(c) Find the radius of a sphere that weighs 192 g.

12 y is proportional to the square root of x. When $x = 25$, $y = 20$.
(a) Find an equation connecting x and y.
(b) Calculate y when $x = 9$.
(c) Calculate x when $y = 100$.

Example

y is inversely proportional to x and $y = 3$ when $x = 5$.
(a) Find an equation connecting x and y.
(b) Calculate y when $x = 2$.
(c) Calculate x when $y = 4$.

(a) $y \propto \frac{1}{x}$ so $y = \frac{k}{x}$. Substituting $y = 3$, $x = 5$,
$3 = \frac{k}{5}$, $k = 15$
$y = \frac{15}{x}$
(b) $y = \frac{15}{2} = 7.5$
(c) $4 = \frac{15}{x}$, $4x = 15$, $x = 3.75$

Example

Repeat the above example if y is proportional to x^2.

(a) $y \propto x^2$ so $y = kx^2$ $3 = k \times 25$, $k = \frac{3}{25}$
$y = \frac{3}{25}x^2$
(b) $y = \frac{3}{25} \times 4 = \frac{12}{25}$
(c) $4 = \frac{3}{25}x^2$, $x^2 = \frac{100}{3}$, $x = \pm 5.77$

Here is an exam question   ...and its solution

The wavelength (L metres), of radio waves, is inversely proportional to the frequency (F kHz). The table below shows some radio stations with their frequencies and wavelengths.

Radio station	Frequency (F)	Wavelength (L)
Radio Atlantic	252 kHz	1179 m
Virgin Radio	1215 kHz	
BBC World Service		458·5 m

(a) Express L in terms of F.

(b) Calculate the wavelength of Virgin Radio to the nearest metre.

(c) Calculate the frequency of the BBC World Service.

(a) $L = \dfrac{297\,108}{F}$

$L \propto \dfrac{1}{F}$ so $L = \dfrac{K}{F}$,

$1179 = \dfrac{K}{252}$,

$K = 1179 \times 252 = 297\,108$

(b) $245\,\text{m}$

$L = \dfrac{297\,108}{1215}$

(c) $648\,\text{kHz}$

$458·5 = \dfrac{297\,108}{F}$,

$458·5F = 297\,108$,

$F = 297\,108 \div 458·5$

Now try these exam questions:

1 Kelly invested $450 for three years at 6% per year compound interest.
Calculate the total amount that the investment was worth at the end of the three years.

2 In 1995 Mr and Mrs Mann paid $160·48 for their house insurance. The cost of insurance rose by 2·5% each year. How much did they pay in 1998?

3 The time of swing, T seconds, of a pendulum is proportional to the square root of the length, L centimetres, of the pendulum. A pendulum of length 64 cm has a time of swing of 1·6 seconds. Find the formula for T in terms of L.

4 The amount of sag, S cm, when a beam is carrying a load at its midpoint, is proportional to the cube of its length, L m. The amount of sag is 2·4 cm for a beam of length 4 m.

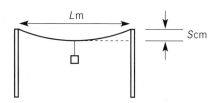

(a) Find a formula for S in terms of L.
(b) What is the amount of sag for a beam of length 6 m?
(c) For another beam the amount of sag is 0·3 cm. What is the length of this beam?

5 P is **inversely proportional** to the **square root** of Q. If $P = 12$ when $Q = 49$, find an expression for P in terms of Q.

Calculator methods

Calculators vary. The position and symbols used on the buttons are different depending on the make and model of calculator. The order in which the buttons have to be pressed can also vary. Make sure you know how **your** calculator works. Don't borrow a different calculator or change your calculator just before an exam.

Calculating with negative numbers

Use $[(-)]$ or $[+/-]$ to make negative numbers.

Don't get $[(-)]$ and $[-]$ confused.

Now try these:

1 Work out the following.
  (a) $5 \times {}^-2$ (c) ${}^-30 \div 4$ (e) $7 - ({}^-5)$
  (b) ${}^-6 + ({}^-3)$ (d) ${}^-6 \times {}^-6$ (f) ${}^-9 + 5$

Example

Work out the following.
(a) ${}^-3 \times {}^-5$ (b) $5 - ({}^-3)$

(a) $[(-)]\,[3]\,[\times]\,[(-)]\,[5]\,[=]\ 15$
or, on some calculators
$[3]\,[+/-]\,[\times]\,[5]\,[+/-]\,[=]\ 15$
(b) $[5]\,[-]\,[(-)]\,[3]\,[=]\ 8$

Calculating with fractions

Use the $[a^b/c]$ button.

Now try these:

2 Change these fractions into their simplest form.
  (a) $\frac{20}{35}$ (b) $\frac{21}{27}$ (c) $\frac{31}{42}$

3 Work out the following.
  (a) $\frac{4}{5} + \frac{2}{3}$ (c) $1\frac{1}{2} \times 3\frac{3}{8}$
  (b) $4\frac{5}{6} - 2\frac{1}{4}$ (d) $2\frac{2}{3} \div 2\frac{2}{5}$

4 (a) Work out $\frac{3}{4}$ of \$124.
  (b) How many pieces of pipe, $2\frac{3}{4}$ metres long, can be cut from a 55 metre length?

Example

(a) Write $\frac{25}{100}$ as a fraction in its simplest form.
(b) Find $1\frac{2}{3} + \frac{3}{4}$.
(c) Find $\frac{2}{5}$ of \$12.

(a) $[25]\,[a^b/c]\,[100]\,[=]\ \frac{1}{4}$
(b) $[1]\,[a^b/c]\,[2]\,[a^b/c]\,[3]\,[+]\,[3]\,[a^b/c]\,[4]\,[=]\ 2\frac{5}{12}$
(c) $[2]\,[a^b/c]\,[5]\,[\times]\,[12]\,[=]\ 4,4,5 = \$4\cdot80$

Notice how the answer of $4\frac{4}{5}$ becomes \$4·80.

Reciprocals

Use the $[1/x]$ or the $[x^{-1}]$ button.

Now try these:

5 Find the reciprocal of these.
  (a) 8   (c) 0·04
  (b) $\frac{4}{5}$ (d) $2\frac{3}{4}$

Example

Work out the reciprocal of the following.
(a) 0·1   (b) $1\frac{2}{3}$

(a) $[0]\,[\cdot]\,[1]\,[1/x]\,[=]\ 10$
(b) $[1]\,[a^b/c]\,[2]\,[a^b/c]\,[3]\,[1/x]\,[=]\ \frac{3}{5}$

$0\cdot6 = \frac{3}{5}$

Powers and roots

• Use $[x^y]$ or $[\wedge]$ for powers.
• Use $[x^{1/y}]$ or $[\wedge]$ with (a ÷ b) for roots.

Now try these:

6 Work out the following.
  (a) 5^4 (c) $81^{\frac{1}{4}}$
  (b) $6^4 - 4^6$ (d) $\sqrt[5]{243}$ (e) $100^{-\frac{5}{2}}$

Example

Work out these.
(a) 6^7 (b) $4^5 + 3^4$ (c) $100^{-\frac{1}{2}}$ (d) $1024^{\frac{4}{5}}$

Your calculator may require you to press $[(-)]$ or $[+/-]$ after 2.

(a) $[6]\,[x^y]\,[7]\,[=]\ 279\,936$
(b) $[4]\,[\wedge]\,[5]\,[+]\,[3]\,[\wedge]\,[4]\,[=]\ 1105$
(c) $[100]\,[x^{1/y}]\,[(-)]\,[2]\,[=]\ 0\cdot1$
(d) $[1024]\,[\wedge]\,[(]\,[4]\,[\div]\,[5]\,[)]\,[=]\ 256$

Brackets

When doing complex calculations with a calculator, be safe and introduce brackets. Remember that for every [(] there must be a [)].

Now try these:

7 Work out the following.

(a) $\dfrac{3\cdot6 \times 5\cdot9}{2\cdot47 - 1\cdot98}$

(b) $3\cdot2^2 - \sqrt{4\cdot84}$

(c) $5\cdot8 \times 1\cdot7 + 3\cdot5 \times 4\cdot4$

(d) $\dfrac{26\cdot9 - 7\cdot8}{\sqrt{8} + 1\cdot95}$

Example

Work out these.

(a) $\dfrac{2\cdot3 + 4\cdot5}{5 \times 3\cdot2}$

(b) $6\cdot4 + 7\cdot2 \times 8$

(a) [(] [2] [.] [3] [+] [4] [.] [5] [)] [÷]
[(] [5] [×] [3] [.] [2] [)] [=] 0·425

(b) [6] [.] [4] [+] [(] [7] [.] [2] [×] [8] [)] [=] 64

Standard form

Use [EXP] or [EE].
These are **in place of** [×] [1] [0] in a standard form number.

Now try these:

8 Work out these.

(a) $4\cdot25 \times 10^{-2} \times 1\cdot72 \times 10^{-3}$

(b) $(3\cdot7 \times 10^5)^2$

(c) $\dfrac{3\cdot4 \times 10^6}{5 \times \sqrt{0\cdot0289}}$

Your calculator may not give the answer in standard form.

Example

Work out the following.

(a) $2\cdot3 \times 10^6 + 5 \times 10^7$

(b) $\dfrac{6\cdot2 \times 10^8 - 7\cdot5 \times 10^7}{1\cdot5 \times 10^3}$

Give your answer in standard form.

(a) [2] [.] [3] [EXP] [6] [+] [5] [EXP] [7] [=] $5\cdot23 \times 10^7$

(b) [(] [6] [.] [2] [EXP] [8] [–] [7] [.] [5] [EXP] [7] [)]
[÷] [1] [.] [5] [EXP] [3] [=] $3\cdot63 \times 10^5$

Trigonometric keys

Use the [sin] [cos] and [tan] keys.
Before using these always check that your calculator is in degree mode, [DEG] or [D].

Now try these:

9 Work out these.

(a) $5\cos60°$

(b) $\dfrac{50\sin30°}{\sin80°}$

(c) $10\cos47° + 25\sin43°$

Example

Work out the following.

(a) $\sin30° + \cos60°$

(b) $\dfrac{4 + \tan45°}{5^2}$

(a) [sin] [30] [+] [cos] [60] [=] 1 on some calculators
or
[30] [sin] [+] [60] [cos] [=] 1

(b) [(] [4] [+] [tan] [45] [)] [÷] [5] [x^2] [=] 0·2

Here is an exam question   ...and its solution

Work out the following. Give your answers to 2 d.p.

(a) $4\cdot2^4$

(b) $\dfrac{3\cdot9^2 + 0\cdot53}{3\cdot9 \times 0\cdot53}$

(c) $\sqrt{(3 + 5\cos40°)}$

(a) 311·17

(b) 7·61

(c) 2·61

Now try these exam questions:

1 Find:

(a) $\frac{3}{5}$ of 200 g

(b) $2\frac{3}{4} - 1\frac{4}{5}$

(c) $\frac{4}{7}$ of $26·60.

2 Work out the reciprocal of 3^2.

3 Work out these.

(a) $\dfrac{18\cdot6 - 2\cdot75}{3\cdot5 + 1\cdot043}$

(b) $\dfrac{1}{4\cdot5 + 6\cdot8}$

(c) $3\cdot2\left(5\cdot2 - \frac{1}{1\cdot6}\right)$

4 Work out these.

(a) $\dfrac{4\cdot25 - 1\cdot7^4}{1\cdot25^2}$

(b) $\sqrt{(3^2 + 2\cdot7^3)}$

5 Work out these.

(a) $6\cdot3 \times 10^9 + 5\cdot8 \times 10^{10}$

(b) $\dfrac{(9\cdot52 \times 10^{14})^2}{8 \times 10^{-3}}$

6 Work out these.

(a) $6(\cos27° + \sin27°)$

(b) $3 - 4\sin28\cdot7°$

7 Work out $64^{\frac{4}{3}}$.

Solving problems

Some common money problems

You need to be able to:
- assess value for money
- deal with other ratio problems
- calculate currency exchange
- calculate tax/insurance
- work out percentage problems.

Now try these:

1 Three families share the cost of a meal in the ratio 2 : 3 : 4. The total cost of the meal was $72. How much did each family pay?

2 Jenny had to pay 10% tax on $1520 of her income, and 22% tax on $1435. How much tax did she pay altogether?

Example
A spade costing $13·60 was reduced by 15% in a sale. Find its sale price.

Sale price = 85% of $13·60
= 0·85 × $13·60 = $11·56

Make sure you know what the percentage is 'of' – watch out for reverse percentage problems.

3 Nassim's yearly pay after a 3% rise was $16 995. What was his yearly pay before the increase?

Always show enough working to make your methods clear.

Compound measures

Examples are:
- speed
- density
- population density.

Now try these:

4 Pali drives 270 kilometres in 4 hours 30 minutes. Find his average speed in kilometres per hour.

5 A gold ring has a mass of 15·44 g and a volume of 0·8 cm^3. Find its density.

The units tell you which way to divide, so density measured in g/cm^3 means grams (mass) divided by cm^3 (volume).

6 A town has a population density of 2530 people/km^2 and an area of 87 km^2. Find the population of the town.

Checking your work

Use the following methods:
- common sense – is the answer reasonable?
- inverse operations – work backwards to check
- estimates – one significant figure is often easiest.

Example
Pat calculated $\frac{67·4 \times 504·9}{12·3}$ and got the answer 418 572·2
Use estimates to show her answer is wrong.

$\frac{70 \times 500}{10} = 3500$ Her answer is far too large.

(In fact, Pat had multiplied by mistake instead of dividing.)

Accuracy of answers

- Sometimes you are asked to round to a given accuracy – either to a given number of decimal places, or to a given number of significant figures.
- Sometimes you need to work to a reasonable degree of accuracy.

If the value of the first digit being ignored is 5 or more, round up.

Look at the context and the accuracy of the information you have been given.

Now try these:

7 Use 1 s.f. estimates to find approximate answers, showing your estimates.

(a) $792 \div 19$

(b) $\dfrac{5857}{62 \times 20.3}$

8 Round these to 2 d.p.

(a) 30·972   (b) 4·1387   (c) 24·596

9 Round these to 3 s.f.

(a) 5347   (b) 61·42   (c) 3049·6

Trial and improvement

Only use trial and improvement if there is no exact method. Show your trials and their outcomes clearly. For each trial, think what the outcome has told you to try next.

Now try these:

10 The difference of two numbers is 5. Their product is 32·19. Use trial and improvement to find the two numbers.

Here is an exam question   ...and its solution

In June 1998 the speed limit on the Kingston bypass was reduced from 70 to 50 km/h. The bypass is 7·3 kilometres long. How much longer does it take to drive along the bypass at 50 km/h than it did at 70 km/h? Show your method clearly and give your answer in minutes to 1 d.p.

Read the question carefully and break the problem down into steps:
• What do I know?
• What do I have to find?
• What methods can I apply?

$$\text{Time} = \frac{\text{distance}}{\text{average speed}}$$

At 70 km/h

$$\text{time} = \frac{7.3}{70} = 0.1042... \text{ h}$$

At 50 km/h

$$\text{time} = \frac{7.3}{50} = 0.146 \text{ h}$$

Difference $= 0.146 - 0.1042...$ h
$= 0.0417...$ h
$= 0.0417... \times 60$ minutes
$= 2.5$ minutes to 1 d.p.

Now try these exam questions:

1 Sasha, John and Dario went to a restaurant. They agreed to split the cost in the ratio 4 : 3 : 5.
  (a) The food cost $58·80. How much did Dario pay?
  (b) They paid for the drinks in the same ratio. John paid $5·49. How much did Sasha pay?

2 Frankie invested $4000 in a high interest savings account. The rate of compound interest was 7% per annum. She left the money in the account for three years.
  (a) How much was in Frankie's account at the end of the three years?
  (b) She decides to leave all the money in the account. After how many **more** years will there be more than $8000 in the account?

3 Liam drove from Ambridge to Dorchester, a distance of 180 kilometres. He drove the first 90 kilometres at an average speed of 60 km/h, had a 50 minute break and then drove the rest of the distance in 1 hour 40 minutes. What was his average speed for the journey, including the break?

4 The table shows the population of three countries.
  (a) Calculate the total population of the three countries. Give your answer to a reasonable degree of accuracy.
  (b) The area of Denmark is 43 000 square kilometres. Calculate the average number of people per square mile in Denmark.

Country	Population
Spain	3.92×10^7
Denmark	5.14×10^6
Luxembourg	3.73×10^5

5 Leah received a bonus of $900 in 1999. This was a 20% increase on her bonus in 1998. How much was her bonus in 1998?

6 When a tuned guitar string is plucked, it vibrates and produces a musical note. The frequency of the note produced is inversely proportional to the vibrating length of the string. When this length is 40 cm a note of frequency 165 Hz is produced. Calculate the length of string needed to produce a note of frequency 147 Hz.

Symbols, indices, factors and expansions

Forming equations

Everyday problems can often be solved by using letters and writing an equation.

In an exam you must use an equation even if you can work out the answer without. Use it as a check.

Now try these:

1 The length of a rectangle is 4 cm longer than its width. The perimeter is 40 cm. Set up an equation and solve it to find the length and width.

2 At a meeting there were ten more men than women. There were 58 people altogether. Use algebra to work out the number of men and women.

3 A number is squared and 8 added. The result is 89. Set up an equation and solve it to find the number.

Example

In a triangle, one angle is twice the size of the smallest angle, and the third angle is 20° larger than the smallest angle. Write down an equation and solve it to find the three angles.

Let the smallest angle be a, one angle be $2a$ and the other $a + 20$.

So $a + 2a + a + 20 = 180$
$$4a = 160$$
$$a = 40$$

Angles are 40°, 80°, 60°.

Multiplying brackets by single terms

When expanding a single bracket, multiply every term within the bracket by the term immediately in front of the bracket.

Now try these:

Expand and simplify.

4 $a(2a - 3) + 2a(3a + 2)$ 6 $4(2x - 3y) - 2(x + y)$

5 $3x(2x + 3) - 4x(x - 3)$ 7 $3x + 2x(x - 2)$

Example

Expand and simplify $3(2a + 3b) - 2(a - 2b)$.

$= 6a + 9b - 2a + 4b$ $-2 \times -2b = +4b$
$= 4a + 13b$

Collect like terms.

Multiplying two brackets

When expressions of the form $(a + b)(2a - 3b)$ are expanded, every term in the first bracket is multiplied by every term in the second bracket.

'Multiply out', 'expand' and 'remove the brackets' all mean the same thing.

Now try these:

Multiply out the brackets.

8 $(x + 3)(2x - 2)$ 11 $(a - 3b)(a + 2b)$

9 $(2x - 1)(3x - 2)$ 12 $(y - 2)(y + 2)$

10 $(x - 3)(5x + 4)$ 13 $(4x + 5)^2$

Example

Multiply out the brackets.
(a) $(3a + 5)(4a - 3)$
(b) $(x - 3)^2$

(a) $3a(4a - 3) + 5(4a - 3)$
$= 12a^2 - 9a + 20a - 15$
$= 12a^2 + 11a - 15$
(b) $(x - 3)(x - 3)$
$= x(x - 3) - 3(x - 3)$ Multiply the bracket by itself.
$= x^2 - 3x - 3x + 9$
$= x^2 - 6x + 9$

Common factors

Look for every number or letter that is common to every term and write these outside a bracket. Write the terms in the bracket needed to give the original expression when expanded.

Example

Factorise these.
(a) $3a + 6$
(b) $2x^2 - 3xy$
(c) $4a - 8ac + 16a^2b$

$4a = 4a \times 1$ so 1 must be in the bracket.

(a) $3(a + 2)$
(b) $x(2x - 3y)$
(c) $4a(1 - 2c + 4ab)$

Now try these:

Factorise these.

14 $5x - 25$

16 $3ab - 2ac$

15 $2a^2b - 6ab^2$

17 $4abc - 8ab + 2a$

Factorising by grouping

Factorising can be seen as the reverse of expanding brackets.

Now try these:

Factorise these.

18 $10x + 2xy + 3y + 15$

19 $2x + 3xy + 9y + 6$

20 $8x + 6xy + 12 + 9y$

21 $4b + 3ab + 20 + 15a$

22 $7ab + 14a + 6 + 3b$

23 $9ab + 4 + 6a + 6b$

24 $3x + 2xy - 15 - 10y$

25 $2xy + 3x - 12 - 8y$

26 $6x - 9xy + 8 - 12y$

27 $8 - 3ab + 6b - 4a$

Example

Factorise $12x + 16 + 3xy + 4y$.

There is no common factor of each of these terms so you need to look for pairs of terms that will factorise.

$(12x + 16) + (3xy + 4y)$

Factorise each bracket separately.

$= 4(3x + 4) + y(3x + 4)$

Notice that $(3x + 4)$ is a common factor of the two new terms and factorise again.

$= (3x + 4)(4 + y)$

You can always check that your answer is correct by expanding it.

It is possible to group the terms differently and still get the same answer.

$(12x + 3xy) + (16 + 4y)$
$= 3x(4 + y) + 4(4 + y)$
$= (3x + 4)(4 + y)$

Difference of two squares

This can be checked by expanding the brackets.
$(a - b)(a + b)$
$= a^2 - ab + ab - b^2$
$= a^2 - b^2$

- You should know that $a^2 - b^2$ factorises to $(a - b)(a + b)$
- It can be seen from this that when factorising an expression that is a 'difference of two squares' the outcome has the same terms in each bracket with one sign − and the other +.

Example

Factorise $x^2 - 16y^2$

$(x - 4y)(x + 4y)$ — Both of the terms are squares.

Example

Factorise $5x^2 - 20y^2$

Neither of the terms is square but there is a common factor, factorise the expression.

$5(x^2 - 4y^2)$

The terms in the bracket are both squares, factorise.

$= 5(x - 2y)(x + 2y)$

Now try these:

Factorise these.

28 $x^2 - y^2$

33 $r^2 - 16s^2$

29 $p^2 - q^2$

34 $2a^2 - 8b^2$

30 $v^2 - w^2$

35 $16m^2 - 36n^2$

31 $x^2 - 4y^2$

36 $5x^2 - 20y^2$

32 $9a^2 - b^2$

37 $x^6 - y^2$

Indices

- You need to know the rules of indices. They are:

$a^m \times a^n = a^{m+n}$ $\qquad a^m \div a^n = a^{m-n}$

$(a^m)^n = a^{m \times n}$ $\qquad a^0 = 1$

$\dfrac{1}{a^n} = a^{-n}$ $\qquad a^{\frac{1}{2}} = \sqrt{a}$ $\qquad a^{\frac{1}{3}} = \sqrt[3]{a}$

- The rules of indices also need to be used to manipulate expression involving letters and numbers.

- Remember $a = a^1$.

Now try these:

Write these as whole numbers or fractions.

38 2^3

40 $\left(\frac{1}{3}\right)^{-2}$

39 $25^{\frac{1}{2}}$

41 $4^{\frac{3}{2}}$

Simplify these.

42 $2abc^2 \times 4ab^2c$

44 $(4a^2)^3$

43 $\dfrac{14a^2b^3}{2a^3b}$

45 $\dfrac{4a \times 3b^2}{2a^2b}$

Numbers are $5 \times 4 \div 12 = \frac{5}{3}$.

Letters are $a^{2-3} = a^{-1}$ or $\frac{1}{a}$ and $b^{1+3-2} = b^2$.

Example

Write these as whole numbers or fractions.

(a) $8^{\frac{1}{3}}$ **(b)** 2^{-3} **(c)** 4^0 **(d)** $27^{\frac{2}{3}}$

(a) 2 — Find the cube root.

(b) $\frac{1}{8}$

(c) 1 — Invert and cube.

(d) 9 — Find cube root and then square.

Example

Simplify these.

(a) $3a^7b^2 \times 4ab^3$ **(b)** $\dfrac{5a^2b \times 4b^3}{12a^3b^2}$ **(c)** $(2a^2b)^3$

(a) $12a^3b^5$ — The numbers are multiplied and the indices added.

(b) $\dfrac{5b^2}{3a}$

(c) $8a^6b^3$ — The number is cubed and the indices are multiplied by 3.

Here is an exam question   ...and its solution

(a) Expand $(2q - 3)(q + 5)$.

(b) Factorise completely $6p^2 - 8p$.

(c) Simplify $\dfrac{2a^4 \times 4a^2}{a^3}$.

(d) Find the value of $\left(\dfrac{49}{4}\right)^{-\frac{3}{2}}$ as a fraction.

(a) $2q^2 + 7q - 15$

(b) $2p(3p - 4)$

(c) $8a^3$

(d) $\dfrac{8}{343}$

$2q(q + 5) - 3(q + 5) =$
$2q^2 + 10q - 3q - 15$

Invert, find the square root and cube.

Now try these exam questions:

1 Factorise completely $12p^2q - 15pq^2$.

2 Multiply out and simplify these.
  (a) $2(3x + 1) - 4(x - 3)$ **(b)** $(3 - x)^2$

3 Simplify these.
  (a) $3s^2 + 2s - 4s + s^2 - 5$
  (b) $(2e - f)(e + 3f)$
  (c) $\dfrac{12p^2q}{3p} \times 2q^2$

4 Large radiators cost \$45 more than small radiators. Glen buys three small and two large radiators for \$415. Write down an equation and solve it to find the cost of a small radiator.

5 (a) Simplify $\dfrac{3a^2b \times 4a^2}{2a^3b}$.
  (b) Factorise completely $4a^2 - 2a$.

6 Simplify the following expression.
  $\left(\sqrt{a} + \sqrt{b}\right)\left(\sqrt{a} - \sqrt{b}\right)$

7 Simplify these.
  (a) $3a^2b \times 4ab^3$
  (b) $\dfrac{14a^3b^2}{2ab^3}$

8 Expand these.
  (a) $(3x - 2)(x + 4)$
  (b) $(2y - 1)(y - 3)$

9 Factorise these.
  (a) $15a - 9 - 10ab + 6b$
  (b) $3a - 6 + 10b - 5ab$

10 Factorise these.
  (a) $50a^2 - 18b^2$
  (b) $x^4 - y^4$

11 (a) Work out the exact value of $2^{-3} \times 16^{\frac{1}{2}}$.
  (b) Simplify as far as possible $\sqrt{p^4q^{-3}} \times \sqrt{\dfrac{q}{p^{-2}}}$.

12 (a) Factorise $ab^2 - 3a^2b$.
  (b) Find the value of $9^{-1} \times 27^{\frac{2}{3}}$.

Linear equations

Solving equations

Always perform the same operation on each side of the equation.

Now try these:

1 $5x + 6 = 31$

2 $4p + 4 = 12$

3 $4m = 9$

4 $7y - 6 = 50$

Example

Solve the equation $3x - 4 = 20$.

First add 4 to both sides giving:
$3x - 4 + 4 = 20 + 4$

> This line can be left out.

$$3x = 24$$

Then divide each side by 3 giving:
$$x = \frac{24}{3} = 8$$

Brackets in equations

If the equation has brackets multiply out the brackets first.

Now try these:

Solve the following equations.

5 $2(m - 4) = 10$

6 $5(p + 6) = 40$

7 $7(x - 2) = 42$

> The answer is negative in question 8.

8 $3(4 - x) = 21$

Example

Solve $3(x + 4) = 24$.

$$3(x + 4) = 24$$
$$3x + 12 = 24$$
$$3x = 12$$
$$x = 4$$

Dealing with the 'unknown'

If the 'unknown' is on both sides of the equation rearrange to collect the numbers on one side and the unknown on the other side.

Now try these:

Solve the following equations.

9 $7x - 4 = 3x + 8$

10 $6x - 2 = x + 10$

11 $3x + 2 = 8x + 1$

> The answer is negative in question 12.

12 $5x + 2 = 7x + 10$

Example

Solve $5x + 4 = 2x + 19$.

First subtract 4 from each side:
$5x = 2x + 15$

Then subtract $2x$ from each side:
$3x = 15$
$x = 5$

More than one set of brackets

If there are more than one set of brackets multiply them out first.

Now try these:

Solve the following equations.

> The answer is negative in question 13.

13 $6(x + 4) = 4(x - 3)$

14 $7(m - 2) = 5(m + 4) + 12$

15 $4(p + 2) = 5(p - 5) - 9$

16 $3(4x - 4) = 4(2x + 8)$

Example

Solve $5(2x + 1) = 4(x - 2) + 10$.

$$5(2x + 1) = 4(x - 2) + 10$$
$$10x + 5 = 4x - 8 + 10$$
$$10x = 4x - 8 + 10 - 5$$
$$= 4x - 3$$
$$6x = {}^{-}3$$
$$x = \frac{{}^{-}3}{6} = \frac{{}^{-}1}{2}$$

Fractions in equations

If the equation has a fraction in it multiply both sides of the equation by the denominator.

Example

(a) $\frac{3x}{4} = 12$

(b) $\frac{2}{3}(x + 2) = 4$

(c) $\frac{3}{4}(2 - x) = \frac{1}{5}(2x - 1)$

(a) Multiply both sides by 4 giving:
$$3x = 48$$
so $x = \frac{48}{3} = 16.$

(b) Multiply both sides by 3 giving:
$$2(x + 2) = 12$$
$$2x + 4 = 12$$
$$2x = 8$$
$$x = 4$$

(c) Multiply both sides by 20 giving:
$$15(2 - x) = 4(2x - 1)$$
$$30 - 15x = 8x - 4$$
$$23x = 34$$
$$x = \frac{34}{23}$$
$$= 1\frac{11}{23}$$

Now try these:

17 $\frac{x}{4} = 4$

18 $\frac{3x}{4} = 6$

> Multiply by 4 and by 5, that is, multiply by 20.

19 $\frac{1}{2}(x + 7) = 4$

20 $\frac{1}{5}(2x - 1) = 3$

21 $\frac{1}{2}(x + 1) = \frac{1}{3}(2x - 1)$

22 $\frac{3}{4}x - 2 = \frac{x}{3}$

Here is an exam question   ...and its solution

Solve the following equations.

(a) $\frac{5x + 8}{3} = 6$

(b) $4(x + 7) = 3(2x - 4)$

(a) $x = 2$
$$\frac{5x + 8}{3} = 6$$
$$5x + 8 = 18$$
$$5x = 10$$
$$x = 2$$

(b) $x = 20$
$$4(x + 7) = 3(2x - 4)$$
$$4x + 28 = 6x - 12$$
$$40 = 2x$$
$$x = 20$$

Now try these exam questions:

1 Solve $3x = x + 1$.

2 Solve $3p - 4 = p + 8$.

3 Solve $\frac{3m}{4} = 9$.

4 Solve $2(y + 3) = 5y$.

5 Solve $4(x - 1) = 2x + 3$.

6 Solve $4(x + 2) + 2(3x - 2) = 14$.

7 A rectangle has its longer side 2 cm more than its shorter side. Its perimeter is 36 cm.
   Let x cm be the length of the shorter side.
   (a) Write down an equation in x.
   (b) Solve your equation to find x.
   (c) Find the area of the rectangle.

Formulae

Substituting in formulae

- Remember expressions like ab mean $a \times b$.
- Multiplication and division are done before addition and subtraction unless brackets tell you otherwise.
- Expressions like $3r^2$ mean $3 \times r^2$ – that means you square r and then multiply by 3.

> Don't forget $3x^2$ means $3 \times x^2$.

Now try these:

1 If $A = 3x^2 - 5y^2$, find A when $x = 4$ and $y = \;^-3$.

2 If $y = \dfrac{(a + b)h}{2}$, find y when:

   (a) $a = 2.3$, $b = 5.2$ and $h = 1.9$

   (b) $a = \frac{1}{2}$, $b = \frac{3}{4}$ and $h = \;^-3$.

3 If $s = ut + \frac{1}{2}at^2$, find s when $u = 30$, $a = \;^-10$ and $t = 5$.

Example

(a) If $C = 6b + 3a^2$, find C when $b = \;^-3$ and $a = 5$.

(b) If $y = \dfrac{3a - 2b}{c}$, find y when:

   (i) $a = 2$, $b = \;^-5$ and $c = 3$

   (ii) $a = \frac{1}{4}$, $b = \frac{3}{4}$ and $c = 2$

(a) $C = 6 \times \;^-3 + 3 \times 5^2 = \;^-18 + 75 = 57$

(b)(i) $y = \dfrac{3 \times 2 - 2 \times (^-5)}{3} = \dfrac{6 + 10}{3} = 5\frac{1}{3}$

(ii) $y = \dfrac{3 \times \frac{1}{4} - 2 \times \frac{3}{4}}{2} = \dfrac{\frac{3}{4} - 1\frac{1}{2}}{2} = \dfrac{\frac{-3}{4}}{2} = \;^-\frac{3}{8}$

Writing your own formulae

- Make sure you define your letters carefully, including any units.
- Make sure you use brackets if you want addition and subtraction to be done before multiplication and division.
- Use a fraction line not a ÷ sign for divide.

Now try these:

4 To convert from the Fahrenheit scale to Celsius take off 32 and multiply by $\frac{5}{9}$. Write this as a formula.

5 Write a formula for the nth term of these sequences.

   (a) 1, 4, 9, 16, 25 …   **(c)** 2, 5, 8, 11, 14 …

   (b) 3, 12, 27, 48, 75 …   **(d)** 25, 21, 17, 13 …

6 Write a formula for the nth term of these sequences.

   (a) 2, 4, 8, 16, 32 …   **(c)** 2, 5, 10, 17, 26 …

   (b) 5, 10, 20, 40, 80 …

Example

Write a formula for the perimeter of a semicircle.

Let r = the radius in cm and P = the perimeter in cm.

Half the circumference $= \frac{1}{2} \times 2\pi r$

so $P = 2r + \pi r$.

> Remember to define your letters.

> The Fahrenheit scale is used to measure temperature in the USA.

Rearranging formulae

To change the subject of a formula use the same rules as for equations. Do the same thing to both sides to get the new subject on its own on one side of the formula.

Now try these:

Make the letter in square brackets the subject of these formulae.

7 $y = mx + c$ [c]   **10** $x = ab - cd$ [c]

8 $y = mx + c$ [m]   **11** $P = 2(\ell + w)$ [w]

9 $x = ab - cd$ [b]   **12** $V = \frac{1}{3}\ell wh$ [h]

Example

Make u the subject of $s = \dfrac{(u + v)}{2} \times t$.

$2s = (u + v) \times t$ Multiply both sides by 2.

$2s = ut + vt$ Multiply out the brackets.

$2s - vt = ut$ Take vt from both sides.

$\dfrac{2s - vt}{t} = u$ Divide both sides by t.

$u = \dfrac{2s - vt}{t}$ Rewrite with u on the left.

> Remember to always do the same thing to both sides.

Powers of the subject

- If the required subject is raised to a power, e.g. v^2, first make v^2 the subject and then find the square root of both sides.
- For cubes find the cube root, for power four the fourth root and so on.

Example
Make u the subject of $v^2 = u^2 + 2as$

$$v^2 - 2as = u^2 \quad \blacktriangleleft \text{ Take } 2as \text{ from both sides.}$$
$$u^2 = v^2 - 2as \quad \blacktriangleleft \text{ Change the sides.}$$
$$u = \sqrt{v^2 - 2as} \quad \blacktriangleleft \text{ Find the square root of both sides.}$$

Subject in twice

If the required subject is in the formula twice:
- get all the terms involving the subject on one side of the formula and all the other terms on the other side
- take the subject out as a common factor
- divide both sides by the bracket.

Now try these:

Make the letter in square brackets the subject of these formulae.

Question 15 could also be written as 'Find a formula for x in terms of a and y.'

Example
Make x the subject of $ax - by = cx + d$.

$$ax = cx + d + by \quad \blacktriangleleft \text{ Add } by \text{ to both sides.}$$
$$ax - cx = d + by \quad \blacktriangleleft \text{ Take } cx \text{ from both sides.}$$
$$x(a - c) = d + by \quad \blacktriangleleft \text{ Factorise.}$$
$$x = \frac{d + by}{a - c} \quad \blacktriangleleft \text{ Divide both sides by } (a - c)$$

13 $A = 4\pi r^2$ $[r]$

14 $V = \frac{4}{3}\pi r^3$ $[r]$

15 $y = x^2 + a$ $[x]$

16 $y = ax + by$ $[y]$

17 $y = a(x + y)$ $[y]$

18 $ab + cd = ac - bd$ $[c]$

Here is an exam question

Use the formula $F = 2(C + 15)$ to find an expression for C in terms of F.

...and its solution

$$C = \frac{1}{2}(F - 30)$$

$$F = 2(C + 15)$$
$$F = 2C + 30$$
$$2C = F - 30$$
$$C = \frac{1}{2}(F - 30)$$

Now try these exam questions:

1 The price, P cents, of printing n party invitations is given by $P = 120 + 4n$.
   Find a formula for n in terms of P.

2 Using $u = 9$, $t = 48$ and $a = \frac{-1}{4}$, work out the value of s from the formula $s = ut + \frac{1}{2}at^2$.

3 The time, T minutes, for cooking a piece of meat weighing W kilograms is found using the instruction 'Cook for 20 minutes and then add 30 minutes for each kilogram'. Write down a formula for T in terms of W.

4 Given that $V = \frac{1}{3}\pi r^2 h$, express r in terms of V, h and π.

5 Write down the nth term of this sequence.
   1, 4, 7, 10, 13, ...

6 (a) The volume, V, of material inside a tube is given by $V = 25\pi(R^2 - r^2)$.
       Calculate the value of V when $\pi = 3 \cdot 1$,
       $R = 7 \cdot 3$ cm and $r = 5 \cdot 9$ cm.
   (b) Make y the subject of the formula $x = 4y^2 - 3$.

7 Rearrange each of the following to give d in terms of e.

   (a) $e = 5d + 3$

   (b) $\dfrac{3d - 7}{4 + 5d} = e$

8 The formula $f = \dfrac{uv}{u + v}$ is used in the study of light.
   (a) Calculate f when $u = 14 \cdot 9$ and $v = {}^-10 \cdot 2$.
       Give your answer to 3 s.f.
   (b) Express v in terms of u and f.

9 Two people start a rumour. The following table shows the number of people (n) who have heard the rumour after t hours.

t	0	1	2	3	4	5
n	2	6	18	54	162	486

   Write down a formula for n in terms of t.

Direct and inverse proportion

Direct proportion

- In direct proportion both variables change in the same way – either both getting larger or both getting smaller.
- Using symbols direct proportion is written as
  $y \propto x$ or $y \propto x^2$.
- The formulae for these are $y = kx$ or $y = kx^2$ respectively, where k is a constant.

These are the most common direct proportions but you could also meet $y \propto x^3$ and $y \propto \sqrt{x}$.

Example

The value, $\$V$ of a diamond is proportional to the square of its mass W g. A diamond weighing 14 g is worth \$490.
(a) Find the value of a diamond weighing 40 g.
(b) Find the mass of a diamond worth \$6000.

(a) $V \propto W^2$ or $V = kW^2$
  $490 = k \times 14^2$, $k = 2.5$
  So $V = 2.5 \times 40^2$, $V = \$4000$
(b) $6000 = 2.5 \times W^2$,
  $W^2 = 2400$, $W = 48.99$

Now try these:

1 If $y \propto x^3$ and $y = 24$ when $x = 2$, find y when $x = 4$.

2 If $y \propto x$ and $y = 8$ when $x = 20$, find x when $y = 36$.

3 A car uses 14 litres of fuel to travel 80 km. How much fuel will it use to travel 250 km?

4 The area, A cm^2, of a TV screen is proportional to the square of the length of the diagonal, d cm. A TV screen with a diagonal of 15 cm has an area of 110 cm^2. What is the area of a screen with a diagonal of 50 cm?

5 When an object is dropped, the distance, d metres, which it falls in t seconds is proportional to t^2. If $d = 122.5$ m when $t = 5$ seconds calculate d when $t = 7$ seconds.

Inverse proportion

- In inverse proportion when one variable increases the other variable decreases.
- Using symbols inverse proportion is written as
  $y \propto \dfrac{1}{x}$ or $y \propto \dfrac{1}{x^2}$.
- The formulae for these are $y = \dfrac{k}{x}$ or $y = \dfrac{k}{x^2}$ respectively, where k is a constant.

These are the most common inverse proportions but you could also meet $y \propto \dfrac{1}{\sqrt{x}}$.

Example

The volume V of a given mass of gas varies inversely as the pressure, P.
When $V = 2$ m^3, $P = 500$ N/m^2.
(a) Find the volume when the pressure is 400 N/m^2.
(b) Find the pressure when the volume is 5 m^3.

(a) $V \propto \dfrac{1}{p}$ or $V = \dfrac{k}{p}$
  $2 = \dfrac{k}{500}$, $k = 1000$
  So $V = \dfrac{1000}{400} = 2.5$ m^3
(b) $P = \dfrac{k}{V} = \dfrac{1000}{5} = 200$ N/m^2

Now try these:

6 y is inversely proportional to x^2, and $y = 4$ when $x = 1$.
   Find y when $x = 2$.

7 y is inversely proportional to $\sqrt{x}$. $y = 1{\cdot}2$ when $x = 100$.
   (a) Calculate y when $x = 4$.
   (b) Calculate x when $y = 3$.

8 The wavelength of a sound-wave, W m, is inversely proportional to the frequency, F Hz.
   A sound-wave with a frequency of 300 Hz has a wavelength of $1{\cdot}1$ m.
   Calculate the wavelength of a sound-wave with frequency of 660 Hz.

9 The brightness of a light varies inversely as the square of the distance from the source. A lamp has a brightness of
   20 lumens at a distance of 1 metre.
   How bright is it at 10 m?

10 The value of a car is inversely proportional to its age in years.
    My three-year-old car is worth $9500.
    What will it be worth in five years' time?

How old will the car be in five years' time?

Here is an exam question   ...and its solution

From a point h metres above sea level the distance,
d kilometres, to the horizon is given by $d \propto \sqrt{h}$.
When $h = 100$ m, $d = 35$ km.
Find d when $h = 25$.

17·5 km

$d \propto \sqrt{h}$ or $d = k\sqrt{h}$
$35 = k\sqrt{100}$, $k = 3{\cdot}5$
So $d = 3{\cdot}5 \times \sqrt{25}$

Now try these exam questions:

1 The variable y is directly proportional to x^2. Given that $y = 75$ when $x = 5$ find the value of y when $x = 10$.

2 The number of coins, N, that can be made from a given volume of metal is given by $N \propto \dfrac{1}{d^2}$ where d cm
   is the diameter. Given that 8000 coins with a diameter of 2 cm can be made from the volume of metal, how many
   coins with a diameter of 4 cm can made from the same volume?

3 The distance travelled by a car after the brakes are applied is proportional to the square of the initial speed.
   If it takes $12{\cdot}5$ m to stop when travelling at 50 km/h how far will a car travel if its initial speed is 120 km/h?

4 A bullet fired from a gun is slowed down by air resistance. The resistance is proportional to the square of the speed.
   If the resistance is 100 N when the speed is 300 m/s find:
   (a) the resistance when the speed is 600 m/s
   (b) the speed if the resistance is 200 N. Give your answer to 3 s.f.

Simultaneous equations and linear inequalities

Simultaneous equations

To solve simultaneous equations:

Step 1: Make the coefficients of x or y equal by multiplying one or both of the equations. Don't forget to multiply **every** term.

Step 2: Eliminate the term with equal coefficients:
– if the signs are the **s**ame, **s**ubtract
– if the signs are the **d**ifferent, **a**dd.

Step 3: Substitute the value back into (1) or (2) to find the value of the other letter.

Step 4: Write down **both** values as your answer.

Step 5: Check your answer by substituting both values back into the equation not used in Step **3**.

Example

$$2x + 3y = 6 \qquad (1)$$
$$x + y = 4 \qquad (2)$$

Multiply (2) by 2 to make x the same.

$$2x + 3y = 6 \qquad (1)$$
$$2x + 2y = 8 \qquad (2) \times 2$$

$2x$ in both, so subtract the equations.

$$y = {}^-2$$

(2) is easier so use this.

$$x + {}^-2 = 4$$
$$x = 6$$

$$x = 6, y = {}^-2$$

Check in (1).

$$2 \times 6 + 3 \times {}^-2 = 6$$
$$12 - 6 = 6 \checkmark$$

Example

$$3x - 5y = 1 \qquad (1)$$
$$2x + 3y = 7 \qquad (2)$$

This time both equations need to be multiplied. Make y the same by (1) $\times$ 3 and (2) $\times$ 5.

$$9x - 15y = 3$$
$$10x + 15y = 35$$

The signs are different so add.

$$19x = 38$$
$$x = 2$$

Substitute in (2).

$$2 \times 2 + 3y = 7$$
$$3y = 3$$
$$y = 1$$

$$x = 2, y = 1$$

Check in (1).

$$3 \times 2 - 5 \times 1 = 1$$
$$6 - 5 = 1 \checkmark$$

Now try these:

1 Solve these simultaneous equations.

(a) $3x + 2y = 13$
$4x + y = 14$

(b) $2x + y = 7$
$3x - 2y = 28$

(c) $3x - 2y = 8$
$4x + 3y = 5$

(d) $3x - 2y = 7$
$y = 2 - 4x$

(e) $x + y = {}^-1$
$x - y = 6$

(f) $5x - 3y = 29$
$3x + 2y = 6$

Inequalities

- The symbols used are:
  $>$ means greater than
  $<$ means less than
  $\geqslant$ means greater than or equal to
  $\leqslant$ means less than or equal to

- Inequalities are solved using the same rules as when solving equations **except** when dividing or multiplying by a negative number. Then the inequality sign is reversed.

Example

Find the largest integer which satisfies
$4x + 10 < 2x + 14$

$$4x - 2x < 14 - 10$$
$$2x < 4$$
$$x < 2$$
The largest integer value less than two is 1.

Example

Solve the inequality
$4x < 6x + 2$

$$^-2x < 2$$
$$x > ^-1$$

> Divided by $^-2$, so reverse inequality sign.

Example

Solve $x^2 \leqslant 16$.

> Turn the inequaltiy round for the negative solution.

$$x \leqslant 4 \text{ and } x \geqslant {}^-4$$
which may be written $^-4 \leqslant x \leqslant 4$

Example

Solve $^-10 < 2x + 1 \leqslant 15$.

> Subtract 1 from $^-10$ and 15.

$$^-11 < 2x \leqslant 14$$
$$^-5{\cdot}5 < x \leqslant 7$$

Now try these:

2 Solve these inequalities.
  (a) $3x < x + 4$
  (b) $3 - 4x > 6 + x$
  (c) $2(3x - 4) \leqslant 3(4x - 3)$

3 Find the smallest integer value which satisfies
  $3(9 - 4x) < 9 + 6x$.

4 Solve $x^2 \geqslant 25$.

5 Solve $5 < 3 - x < 9$.

Here is an exam question   ...and its solution

(a) A gardener finds that two apple trees and five pear trees cost \$90 and that three apple trees and six pear trees cost \$123.

If the cost of one apple tree is \$$x$ and the cost of one pear tree is \$$y$, write down two equations in x and y. Then solve them to find x and y.

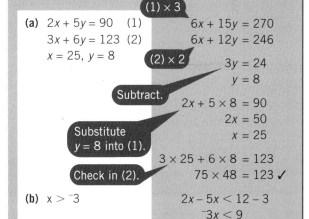

(a) $2x + 5y = 90$ (1)
    $3x + 6y = 123$ (2)
    $x = 25,\ y = 8$

> $(1) \times 3$

$$6x + 15y = 270$$
$$6x + 12y = 246$$

> $(2) \times 2$
> Subtract.

$$3y = 24$$
$$y = 8$$

> Substitute $y = 8$ into (1).

$$2x + 5 \times 8 = 90$$
$$2x = 50$$
$$x = 25$$

> Check in (2).

$$3 \times 25 + 6 \times 8 = 123$$
$$75 \times 48 = 123 \checkmark$$

(b) Solve $2x + 3 < 5x + 12$.

(b) $x > ^-3$

$$2x - 5x < 12 - 3$$
$$^-3x < 9$$
$$x > ^-3$$

Now try these exam questions:

1 Solve these simultaneous equations. $5x + 4y = 13$
                                             $3x + 8y = 5$

2 Solve these simultaneous equations. $4x + 3y = 5$
                                             $2x + y = 1$

3 The equation of the straight line passing through the points (3, 2) and (9, 11) is given by $px + qy = 5$.
  (a) Explain why $3p + 2q = 5$.

(b) Write down another equation in terms of p and q.
(c) Solve the two equations to find the value of p and the value of q.

4 Solve $8x + 5 > 25$.

5 Solve $2x + 17 > 4x + 6$.

6 Solve $x^2 < 36$.

Quadratic equations

Factorising quadratics

To factorise a quadratic, first look at the signs in front of the x-term and the number. The examples cover the four different cases.

> Always multiply out brackets to check.

Example

$x^2 + 5x + 6 = (x + \ )(x + \ )$ | All signs positive.

Find two numbers which add to give 5 and multiply to give 6: 2 and 3

$(x + 2)(x + 3)$

Example

$x^2 + x - 6 = (x + \ )(x - \ )$ | Signs different.

Find two numbers which multiply to give ⁻6 and add to give 1: 3 and ⁻2

$(x + 3)(x - 2)$

Example

$3x^2 - 13x + 4 = (3x - \ )(x - \ )$ | Signs both negative.

Find two numbers which multiply to give 12 (3×4) and add to give ⁻13: ⁻1 and ⁻12

$(3x - 1)(x - 4)$

Example

$2x^2 + x - 3 = (2x \quad)(x \quad)$ | Signs different.

Find two numbers which multiply to give ⁻6 and add to give 1: 3 and ⁻2

$(2x + 3)(x - 1)$

Now try these:

> The signs are different

> Take out the common factor.

1. $x^2 + 6x + 5$
2. $x^2 - 6x + 8$
3. $x^2 - 2x - 15$
4. $x^2 - 9$
5. $3x^2 - 5x + 2$
6. $x^2 - 81$
7. $3x^2 - 27$

Solving quadratic equations by factorising

- If the product of two numbers is 0 then one of the numbers is 0.
- If a quadratic expression equals 0 then one or other of its factors equals 0.

Example

Solve $(x - 2)(x + 3) = 0$

Either $x - 2 = 0$ or $x + 3 = 0$.
So $x = 2$ or $x = ⁻3$.

Example

$x^2 - 3x = 0$
$x(x - 3) = 0$

Then either $x = 0$ or $x - 3 = 0$.
So $x = 0$ or $x = 3$.

Now try these:

Solve these quadratic equations by factorising.

8. $(x - 3)(x - 6) = 0$
9. $(x + 4)(x - 1) = 0$
10. $x^2 + 5x + 4 = 0$
11. $x^2 - 7x + 12 = 0$
12. $x^2 + 3x - 10 = 0$
13. $2x^2 - 13x - 7 = 0$
14. $3x^2 - x - 10 = 0$
15. $6x^2 - 17x + 5 = 0$
16. $x^2 + 4x = 0$
17. $2x^2 - 50 = 0$

Solving quadratic equations that do not factorise

There are two ways of doing this algebraically:

1. Completing the square
   - If the coefficient of x^2 is not 1, divide through the equation by the coefficient of x^2.
   - Make the $x^2 + bx$ terms into a complete square and correct the term added by subtracting $\left(\frac{b}{2}\right)^2$.
   - Rearrange the equation.
   - Take the square root, remembering ±.

Example

Solve $2x^2 - 12x + 1 = 0$.

> Divide by 2.

$x^2 - 6x + 0.5 = 0$
$(x - 3)^2 - 9 + 0.5 = 0$ | $(x - 3)^2 = x^2 - 6x + 9$
$(x - 3)^2 - 8.5 = 0$
$(x - 3)^2 = 8.5$
$x - 3 = \pm \sqrt{8.5}$
$x = 3 \pm \sqrt{8.5}$
$= 5.92$ or 0.08 to 2 d.p.

2 Using the quadratic formula:

When $ax^2 + bx + c = 0$, $x = \dfrac{^-b \pm \sqrt{(b^2 - 4ac)}}{2a}$.

When using this formula, take care with the signs and brackets. Make sure you know how to use your calculator to work it out correctly.

Example

Solve $2x^2 - 7x - 3 = 0$.

$a = 2$, $b = {}^-7$, $c = {}^-3$

$$x = \frac{-\ ^-7 \pm \sqrt{(^-7)^2 - 4 \times 2 \times {}^-3}}{2 \times 2}$$

$$= \frac{7 \pm \sqrt{49 + 24}}{4}$$

$$= \frac{7 \pm \sqrt{73}}{4}$$

$$= 3 \cdot 89 \text{ or } ^-0 \cdot 39 \text{ to 2 d.p.}$$

Now try these:

Try to solve these by completing the square.

18 $x^2 - 4x - 6 = 0$

19 $x^2 + 8x + 2 = 0$

20 $x^2 - 10x + 7 = 0$

21 $x^2 - 3x + 1 = 0$

22 $4x^2 - 8x + 1 = 0$

23 $2x^2 - 4x - 7 = 0$

24 $3x^2 + 12x - 2 = 0$

25 $5x^2 + 30x + 4 = 0$

Try to solve these using the quadratic formula.

26 $x^2 - 5x + 3 = 0$

27 $2x^2 + 8x + 1 = 0$

28 $x^2 - 6x + 4 = 0$

29 $3x^2 - 5x - 1 = 0$

30 $4x^2 - 7x + 2 = 0$

31 $2x^2 - 9x - 7 = 0$

32 $3x^2 + 12x + 2 = 0$

33 $5x^2 + 20x + 4 = 0$

34 Try to solve $x^2 - 4x + 7 = 0$ using the quadratic formula or completing the square. What happens? Draw a graph of

Here is an exam question   ...and its solution

(a) Write $x^2 + 6x + 2$ in the form $(x + a)^2 + b$.

(b) Hence state the minimum value of y on the curve $y = x^2 + 6x + 2$.

(c) Solve the equation $x^2 + 6x + 2 = 0$.

(a) $(x + 3)^2 - 7$

(b) $^-7$

(c) $0 \cdot 35$ or $^-5 \cdot 65$ to 2 d.p.

$x^2 + 6x + 2 = (x + 3)^2 - 9 + 2$

The least value of $(x + 3)^2$ is 0, so the least value of y is 7.

$x^2 + 6x + 2 = 0$
$(x + 3)^2 - 7 = 0$
$(x + 3)^2 = 7$
$x + 3 = \pm\sqrt{7}$
$x = {}^-3 \pm \sqrt{7}$

Now try these exam questions:

1 Solve these equations by factorising.
  (a) $x^2 - 6x + 8 = 0$ **(b)** $2x^2 + 3x - 9 = 0$

2 (a) Factorise completely $5x^2 - 20$.
  (b) (i) Factorise $x^2 - 9x + 8$.
  (ii) Hence solve $x^2 - 9x + 8 = 0$.

3 (a) Multiply out and simplify the expression $(2x + 7)(3x - 6)$.
  (b) (i) Factorise $x^2 + 6x$.
  (ii) Solve the equation $x^2 + 6x = 0$.

4 Solve the equation $2x^2 - 38x + 45 = 0$.

5 (a) Write $3x^2 - 12x + 2$ in the form $3(x - a)^2 - b$.
  (b) Hence solve the equation $3x^2 - 12x + 2 = 0$.

6 The length of a rectangle is y cm, the perimeter is 30 cm and the area is 55 cm².
  (a) Form an equation in y and show that it can be simplified to $y^2 - 15y + 55 = 0$.
  (b) Solve the equation $y^2 - 15y + 55 = 0$ to find the length and width of the rectangle. Give your answers correct to 2 d.p. Do not use a trial and improvement method.

7 Bill is making a rectangular chicken pen against a wall.
The other three sides will be made from wire netting.
Here is the plan:

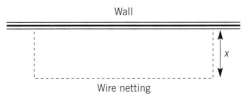

Wall

Wire netting

The total length of wire netting is 22 m.
The area inside the pen must be 60 m².
  (a) Show that $x^2 - 11x + 30 = 0$.
  (b) Solve the equation.
  (c) Describe the size of the pen.

Algebraic fractions

Simplifying fractions

The rules are the same as for numbers.

Example
Simplify the following.

(a) $\dfrac{x^2 + 3x + 2}{x^2 - 1}$　　(b) $\dfrac{1}{x - 1} + \dfrac{1}{x + 2}$

(a) $= \dfrac{(x + 1)(x + 2)}{(x + 1)(x - 1)}$　Factorise the quadratics.

$= \dfrac{x + 2}{x - 1}$　Cancel out common factor.

Common denominator is $(x - 1)(x + 2)$.
Multiply top and bottom by necessary factor.

(b) $= \dfrac{x + 2}{(x - 1)(x + 2)} + \dfrac{x - 1}{(x - 1)(x + 2)}$

$= \dfrac{x + 2 + x - 1}{(x - 1)(x + 2)}$　Combine.

$= \dfrac{2x + 1}{(x - 1)(x + 2)}$

Now try these:

1 $\dfrac{x^2 - x - 2}{x^2 + 2x + 1}$　　2 $\dfrac{2x^2 - 8}{2x^2 - 3x - 2}$　　3 $\dfrac{1}{x} + \dfrac{2}{x - 1}$　　4 $\dfrac{x + 1}{x - 2} - \dfrac{x - 2}{x + 1}$

Solving equations with fractions

Multiply both sides by the common denominator.

Example
Solve $\dfrac{3}{x - 2} - \dfrac{1}{x + 1} = 1$.

$3(x + 1) - (x - 2) = (x - 2)(x + 1)$
$2x + 5 = x^2 - x - 2$
$x^2 - 3x - 7 = 0$
$x = \dfrac{3 \pm \sqrt{9 + 28}}{2} = 4 \cdot 54 \text{ or } ^-1 \cdot 54$

Now try these:

5 $\dfrac{2x}{x - 1} - \dfrac{x + 1}{x + 2} = 0$　　6 $\dfrac{1}{x} + \dfrac{2}{x + 1} = 2$

Here is an exam question　　...and its solution

Michael drives 70 kilometres to work at an average speed of v kilometres per hour.

On the return journey he travels 5 kilometres per hour faster and takes $\frac{1}{4}$ hour less.

(a) (i) Write down expressions in v for the two journey times.
　　(ii) Hence form an equation in v and show that it simplifies to $v^2 + 5v - 1400 = 0$.

(b) Solve the equation to find v.

(a) (i) $\dfrac{70}{v}$ and $\dfrac{70}{v + 5}$

　　(ii) $\dfrac{70}{v} - \dfrac{70}{v + 5} = \dfrac{1}{4}$
　　　　$70(v + 5) - 70v = \dfrac{1}{4}v(v + 5)$
　　　　$1400 = v^2 + 5v$
　　　$v^2 + 5v - 1400 = 0$

(b) $(v - 35)(v + 40) = 0$
　　$v = 35$
　($v = -40$ is not possible.)

Now try these exam questions:

1 (a) Show that the equation $2x - 3 = \dfrac{3(x + 1)}{x + 4}$ can be rearranged to $2x^2 + 2x - 15 = 0$.
　(b) Solve the equation $2x^2 + 2x - 15 = 0$. Give your answer correct to 2 d.p.

2 Simplify this expression as far as possible. $\dfrac{x^2 + 3x}{x^2 + x - 6}$

3 (a) Simplify this expression. $\dfrac{x^2 - 9}{x^2 - x - 6}$
　(b) Use algebra to solve this equation.
　　$\dfrac{12}{3x + 1} - \dfrac{5}{x + 1} = 1$

Sequences

Term-to-term rules

- Every number in a sequence is called a term of the sequence. There is often a simple rule for going from one term to the next.

- Use the term-to-term rule to find the formula for a sequence.

Now try these:

1 Find the first four terms for the sequence given by $3n + 3$.

2 Find the term-to-term rule for the sequence 2, 7, 12, 17... .

3 Find the 15th term and the formula for the nth term for the sequence 5, 11, 17, 23... .

4 Find the formula for the nth term for the sequence 40, 36, 32... .

> In question 4 the nth term is negative.

Example

Here are the first four terms of a sequence: 3, 7, 11, 15.

(a) Find the term-to-term rule.
(b) Find the 20th term.
(c) Find a formula for the nth term of the sequence.

(a) Add 4.
(b) To get the 20th term, add four 19 times.
$3 + 19 \times 4 = 3 + 76 = 79$.
(c) The formula is $3 + (n - 1) \times 4$
$= 3 + 4n - 4 = 4n - 1$.

Common sequences

You should know and recognise common sequences.

Examples

The powers of 2: 1, 2, 4, 8, 16, 32, ... 2^n
The powers of 10: 1, 10, 100, 1000, ... 10^n
The square numbers: 1, 4, 9, 16, ... n^2
The triangle numbers: 1, 3, 6, 10 ... $\dfrac{n(n + 1)}{2}$

Position-to-term rules

- Every number in a sequence can be expressed in terms of its position.

- Use the position-to-term rule to find the formula for the nth term of a sequence:
  - look at the difference between successive terms
  - multiply this difference by n
  - add or subtract a constant to give the required results.

Now try these:

Find a formula for the nth term of each of these sequences.

5 3, 5, 7, 9, ...

6 10, 20, 30, 40, ...

7 ⁻4, 1, 6, 11, ...

8 32, 29, 26, 23, ...

Example

Find the rule for this sequence:
7, 11, 15, 19, ...

It is sometimes useful to write the sequence out in columns:

Position	Term	Difference between terms
1	7	
		4
2	11	
		4
3	15	
		4

This shows that you multiply by 4. The term $4n$ will be in the formula.

Look at position 1. The term is 7.
$4 \times n = 4 \times 1 = 4$
You need to add 3 to give the required result of 7.

Check for position 2.
$4 \times 2 + 3 = 11 \checkmark$

So the nth term $= 4n + 3$.

Other sequences

- Some sequences do not have a common difference between terms. For example if each term is the previous term multiplied by a constant the sequence is a geometric one.

> 'nth term' is also written 'U_n'.

- The rules for other sequences can often be found on inspection.

Example

Find a formula for the nth term of the sequence 4, 20, 100, 500, ...

Each term is $5 \times$ the previous one.
2nd term = 4×5
3rd term = $4 \times 5 \times 5 = 4 \times 5^2$
4th term = $4 \times 5 \times 5 \times 5 = 4 \times 5^3$
nth term = $4 \times 5^{n-1}$

Example

Find a formula for the nth term of the sequence 2×3, 3×4, 4×5, ...

$U_1 = 2 \times 3 = (1 + 1)(1 + 2)$
$U_2 = 3 \times 4 = (2 + 1)(2 + 2)$
$U_n = (n + 1)(n + 2)$

Now try these:

9 Find the formula for the nth term of the following sequences.

   (a) 2, 8, 32, 128, ...   **(b)** 1, 5, 25, 125, ...   **(c)** 3×5, 4×6, 5×7, ...

Here is an exam question   ...and its solution

(a) Write down the 10th term for the sequence 3, 7, 11, 15, ...

(b) Write down an expression for the nth term.

(c) Show that 137 cannot be a term in this sequence.

(a) 39   10th term = $3 + 9 \times 4$

(b) $4n - 1$

Either: the difference between terms is 4 so the expression will start $4n$.
If $n = 1$ then $4n = 4$
therefore subtract 1 to get 3.
Therefore the expression is $4n - 1$.
Or: 1st term is 3, add 4 $(n - 1)$ times, therefore nth term is
$3 + 4(n - 1) = 3 + 4n - 4 = 4n - 1$

(c) If 137 is in the sequence then
$4n - 1 = 137$
therefore $4n = 138$ and $n = 138 \div 4 = 34 \cdot 5$
This is not a whole number.
Therefore 137 cannot be in the sequence.

Now try these exam questions:

1 The first four terms of a sequence are 3, 8, 13, 18. Find the 50th term and nth term of this sequence.

2 The first five terms of a sequence are 1, 6, 11, 16, 21. Find the formula for the nth term.

3 The first four terms of a sequence are 2, 9, 16, 23.
   (a) Find the nth term of this sequence.
   (b) Show that 300 is not in this sequence.

4 **(a)** Write down the formula for the nth term of the sequence 1, 4, 9, 16, 25 ... .
   (b) Hence, or otherwise, find the formula for the nth term of the sequence 4, 13, 28, 49, 76, ...

5 **(a)** Write down the formula for the nth term of the sequence 3, 5, 7, 9, ...
   (b) Hence, or otherwise, find the formula for the nth term of the sequence
      $1 \times 3 + 1$, $2 \times 5 + 1$, $3 \times 5 + 1$, ...

6 The three sequences below are linked. Write down the formula for the nth term of the sequence **(a)**. Use the answer to write down the formula for sequence **(b)** and hence find the formula for the sequence **(c)**.
   (a) 1, 8, 27, 64, ...
   (b) 2, 16, 54, 128, ...
   (c) $^{-}$1, 10, 45, ...

Graphs of linear functions

Gradient and y-intercept

- The gradient of a line is a number indicating how steep it is. The larger the number, the steeper the line.
- Lines with positive gradient slope forwards / , lines with negative gradient slope backwards \ .
- Gradient = $\dfrac{\text{increase in } y}{\text{increase in } x}$.

The y-intercept is the value where the line crosses the y-axis.

Now try these:

1 Find the gradient and y-intercept of each of these lines.

(a) 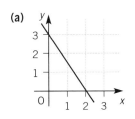   (b)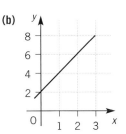

Example
Write down the gradient and y-intercept of these lines.

(a)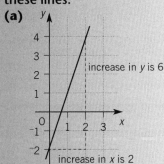

increase in y is 6

increase in x is 2

(b)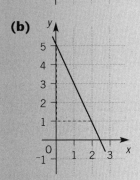

(a) Gradient = $\frac{6}{2}$ = 3   y-intercept = ⁻2

(b) Gradient = $\frac{⁻4}{2}$ = ⁻2   y-intercept = 5

The general equation of a straight line y = mx + c

- In the equation, m stands for the gradient of the line and c is the y-intercept.

- The equation of a line **must** be of the form y = mx + c for the two numbers to represent the gradient and y-intercept.

Example
Write down the equation of each of the lines in the previous example.

(a) y = 3x – 2   (b) y = ⁻2x + 5

Example
Find the gradient and y-intercept of these lines.
(a) y = x + 4
(b) 2y = 6x – 3
(c) 5x – 2y = 12

÷ 2

⁻5x

÷ ⁻2

(a) y = 1x + 4   m = 1, c = 4

(b) y = 3x – 1$\frac{1}{2}$ m = 3, c = ⁻1$\frac{1}{2}$

(c) ⁻2y = ⁻5x + 12
    y = 2$\frac{1}{2}$x – 6   m = 2$\frac{1}{2}$, c = ⁻6

Now try these:

2 Write down the equation of each of the lines in question 1.

3 Work out the gradient, m, and y-intercept, c, for each of the following straight lines.
- **(a)** $y = 4x - 1$
- **(b)** $y = 3 + 2x$
- **(c)** $y = x$
- **(d)** $y + x = 4$
- **(e)** $2y - 3x = 4$
- **(f)** $x - 4y = 10$

4 Find the equation of the line passing through the points
- **(a)** $(1, 0)$ and $(4, 9)$
- **(b)** $(^-2, 9)$ and $(7, ^-9)$.

Example

Find the equation of the line through the points (10, 20) and (30, 30).

$m = \dfrac{30 - 20}{30 - 10} = \dfrac{10}{20} = 0{\cdot}5$

So $y = 0{\cdot}5x + c$
Since line goes through (10, 20),
$20 = 0{\cdot}5 \times 10 + c$
$20 = 5 + c, c = 15$
So equation is $y = 0{\cdot}5\,x + 15$.

Parallel lines

Lines which are parallel have the same gradient.

Example

Find the equation of the line parallel to $y = 2x - 5$ and passing through (0, 4).

From $y = 2x - 5$　　$m = 2$
From $(0, 4)$　　$c = 4$
The equation is　　$y = 2x + 4$.

Now try these:

5 Which of these lines are parallel?
- **(a)** $y = 6x - 2$
- **(b)** $y = 2x - 6$
- **(c)** $6y = 6x - 2$
- **(d)** $6y = 36x - 24$
- **(e)** $y = 6 + x$
- **(f)** $6x - y = 2$

Here is an exam question　　...and its solution

Find the gradient and the equation of the straight line in the diagram.

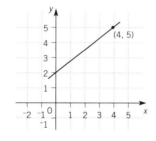

Gradient $= \dfrac{3}{4}$

Equation is $y = \dfrac{3}{4}\,x + 2$.

Now try these exam questions:

1 (a) Work out the gradient of this line.
(b) Write down the equation of the line.

2 (a) Write down the gradient and y-intercept of the line with equation $y = 4 - 2x$.
(b) Write down the equation of the line parallel to $y = 4 - 2x$ which passes through the point $(0, ^-1)$.

3 Find the equation of the straight line which passes through the two points $(^-3, 12)$ and $(5, ^-4)$.

Graphical solution of simultaneous equations and linear inequalities

Graphical solution of simultaneous equations

Simultanous equations can also be solved by graphical methods. The solution is found where the graphs intersect.

- **Step 1:** Work out some values for each equation.

- **Step 2:** Draw the two graphs on the same grid.

- **Step 3:** Find where the two lines cross. Write down the x and y values of the point of intersection.

You can use the same method even if one of the graphs is not a straight line.

Example

Solve graphically $y = 4x - 1$ and $x + y = 4$.

The line $y = 4x - 1$ passes through $(0, {}^-1)$ and $(2, 7)$, and $x + y = 4$ passes through $(0, 4)$ and $(4, 0)$.

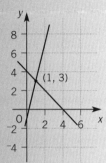

$x = 1,\ y = 3$

Example

Solve graphically $y = x + 1$ and $x^2 + y^2 = 4$.

The line passes through $({}^-1, 0)$ and $(0, 1)$. The circle has centre O and radius 2.

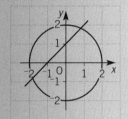

$x = 0 \cdot 8,\ y = 1 \cdot 8$
or
$x = {}^-1 \cdot 8,\ y = {}^-0 \cdot 8$

> Remember to keep the pairs together.

Now try these:

1 Solve these simultaneous equations graphically.
  (a) $y = 2x - 1$
      $y = x + 2$
  (b) $y = 2x - 5$
      $2x + y = 3$

Graphical solution of a set of inequalities

The solution will be represented by a region of the graph.

- **Step 1:** Draw the boundary lines.
  Change the inequality sign to an equals sign.
  Use a continuous line if there is an equals sign in the inequality and a dotted line if there is no equals sign.

Example

Find the region satisfied by
$x \geqslant 1$, $x + y < 5$, and $y \geqslant 2x - 6$.

$x = 1$ is the line through $(1, 0)$ parallel to the y-axis.

The line $x + y = 5$ passes though $(0, 5)$ and $(5, 0)$, and $y = 2x - 6$ passes through $(0, {}^-6)$, $(1, {}^-4)$ and $(2, {}^-2)$.

- **Step 2:** Substitute the coordinates of the origin, (0, 0), to test each inequality.
  If the result is true, shade the opposite side of the line to the origin.
  If the result is false, shade the same side of the line as the origin.

- **Step 3:** The remaining, unshaded area is the region of points satisfying the set of inequalities.

> Shade the unwanted region unless the question states otherwise.

$x \geqslant 1 \Rightarrow 0 \geqslant 1$	**False, shade origin side.**
$x + y < 5 \Rightarrow 0 < 5$	**True, shade opposite side.**
$y \geqslant 2x - 6 \Rightarrow 0 \geqslant {}^-6$	**True, shade opposite side**

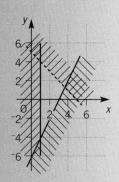

Now try these:

2 Find the region satisfied by each set of inequalities.

(a) $y \leqslant 4$
$x + y \geqslant 4$
$y \geqslant 3x - 1$

(b) $x \leqslant 2$
$2x + 3y \leqslant 12$
$5x + 2y \geqslant 10$

Here is an exam question   ...and its solution

(a) Solve these simultaneous equations graphically.
$y = 3x - 1$
$y = 3 - 2x$

(a)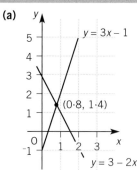

$x = 0.8, y = 1.4$

The line $y = 3x - 1$ passes through
$(0, {}^-1), (1, 2)$ and $(2, 5)$.

The line $y = 3x - 2$ passes through
$(0, 3), (1,1)$ and $(3, {}^-1)$

(b) Write down the three inequalities that satisfy the shaded region.

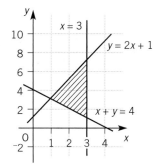

(b) $y \leqslant 2x + 1$
$x \leqslant 3$
$x + y \geqslant 4$

Choose a point in the region: $x = 2, y = 3$.

$y = 2x + 1$
$3 \leqslant 2 \times 2 + 1$
$x = 2 \quad 2 \leqslant 3$
$x + y = 4 \quad 2 + 3 \geqslant 4$

Now try these exam questions:

1 Solve these simultaneous equations graphically.
(a) $y = 3 - x \quad y = 3x - 2$
(b) $y = 3 - x \quad x^2 + y^2 = 25$

2 Solve these simultaneous equations graphically.
$y = 3x + 4 \quad x + y = 2$

3 Find the region satisfied by the inequalities.
$x + y \leqslant 5 \quad y \leqslant 2x - 1 \quad y \geqslant 0$

4 Look at the graph on the right. Write down the three inequalities which satisfy the shaded region.

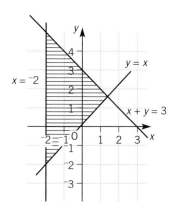

Linear programming

Linear programming

This deals with problems in which a number of simple conditions have to be satisfied at the same time.
There are three steps in solving a problem by linear programming.

- **Step 1:** Set up the inequalities from the information.
- **Step 2:** Draw the graph.
- **Step 3:** Find the solution that best satisfies the requirements.

Setting up inequalities

- Use a letter for each of the two variables and write an inequality for each restriction.
- Often two trivial inequalities, $x \geqslant 0$ and $y \geqslant 0$, are given.

Example

Ahmed buys some doughnuts and some muffins for a party.

Doughnuts cost $1.00 each, and muffins cost $1.50 each.

He wants at least 12 items.

He has $18 to spend.

He wants more muffins than doughnuts.

Write down an inequality to represent each of these three conditions.

Let there be x doughnuts and y muffins.

There must be at least 12 items.

$x + y \geqslant 12$

He can spend up to $18 but no more.

$1.0x + 1.50y \leqslant 18$ — Simplify
$2x + 3y \leqslant 36$

There must be more muffins than doughnuts.

$y > x$

Now try these:

1. A committee must have fewer than 15 members.
   There must be at least five men and at least five women.
   There are x men and y women on the committee.
   Write down three inequalities that x and y must satisfy.

2. Dexters bus company have small buses that seat 24 people and large buses that seat 53 people.
   Julie hires x small buses and y large buses for a trip.
   There are only six drivers available and there are 190 people going on the trip.
   Write down two inequalities that x and y must satisfy.

3. A theatre holds 600 people.
   Adult tickets cost $8 and child tickets cost $5.
   At a performance at least $3200 must be taken to make a profit.
   There must be more adults than children.
   If x children and y adults are at a performance which makes a profit, write down three inequalities that x and y must satisfy.

Graphing the inequalities

- For each inequality draw the line of the associated equation.

  Use a continuous line if the line is included in the required region.

  Use a dotted line if the line is not included in the required region.

- Shade the unwanted region.

Example

Draw axes taking values of both x and y from 0 to 20 and show by shading the region satisfying the inequalities from the previous example.

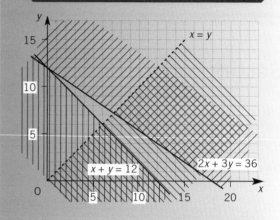

$x + y \geqslant 12$, $2x + 3y \leqslant 36$ and $y > x$.
The inequalities are:

Use continuous line for $x + y = 12$ and $2x + 3y = 36$.

Use a dotted line for $y = x$.

The required region is the unshaded polygon.

Now try these:

For each question, draw and label axes taking values of both x and y from 0 to 12 and show by shading the region satisfied by these inequalities.

4 $y \geqslant 3$, $\qquad$ $4x + 3y \leqslant 36$, $\quad$ $2x > y$

5 $y \geqslant 0$, $\qquad$ $x < 8$, $\qquad$ $y \leqslant x$, $\quad$ $2x + 3y \geqslant 18$

6 $4x + 5y \leqslant 40$, $\quad$ $y \leqslant 3x$, $\qquad$ $y \geqslant 3$

Finding the solution

- Identify the possible solutions in the required region.

- Choose the one which best satisfies the requirements.

Example

In the previous example, find the greatest number of items that can be bought, and the cost.

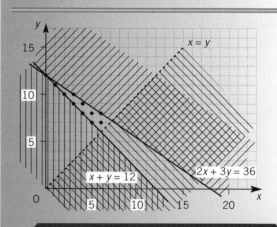

Mark the integer points inside the required region.

Note you do not include (6, 6) or (7, 7) as they are on the dotted boundary.

The greatest number of items is six doughnuts and eight muffins.
These cost \$18.

Now try these:

7 (a) On the graph for question 4, mark all the integer values of (x, y) in the region.

   (b) (i) Find which of these points gives the greatest value of $x + 2y$.

       (ii) State the value.

8 (a) Using the graph for question 5, find the integer value of (x, y) in the region which gives the least value of $2x + 3y$.

   (b) Write down this value.

9 Using the graph for question 6, list the integer values of (x, y) in the region where $x = y$.

Here is an exam question

...and its solution

There are x girls and y boys in a school choir.

(a) (i) The number of girls in the choir is more than 1.5 times the number of boys.
Show that $y < \frac{2x}{3}$.

(ii) There are more than 12 girls in the choir.
There are more than 5 boys in th choir.
The maximum number of children in the choir is 35.
Write down three more inequalities.

(b) (i) Draw axes for $0 \leqslant x \leqslant 40$ and for $0 \leqslant y \leqslant 40$.

(ii) Draw four lines on your graph to represent the inequalities in part (a).
Shade the unwanted parts of the grid.

(c) The school buys a uniform for each choir member.
A girl's uniform costs $25. A boy's uniform costs $20.
Find the maximum possible cost for the choir uniforms.
Mark clearly the point P on your graph which you use to calculate the cost.

Now try these exam questions:

1 A factory produces two types of garden ornaments, type A and type B.
Type A takes 1 hour of machine time and 3 hours of workers' time.
Type B takes 2 hours of machine time and 1 hour of workers' time.
In a day there are 28 hours of machine time and 24 hours of workers' time available.

(a) If x of type A and y of type B are produced in a day, write down two inequalities satisfied by x and y.

(b) Draw these inequalities on a graph, shading the unwanted regions.

(c) The profit made on each type A is $20 and on each type B is $10.
(i) Find the greatest profit that can be made.
(ii) How many of each type are produced to make this profit?

2 A school library is given $1000 for new books. They buy x paperback and y hardback books.
There must be at least 50 books and there must be more hardback than paperback books.
Paperback books cost $10 and hardback books cost $25.

(a) (i) Explain why $2x + 5y \leqslant 200$.
(ii) Write down two more inequalities involving x and y, other than $x \geqslant 0$, $y > 0$.

(b) Represent these inequalities on a graph, shading the unwanted regions.

(c) The school orders the maximum number of hardback books, subject to these conditions.
Find this number from your graph.

3 On a safari trek, there are 60 people and 4500 kg of baggage.
Two types of vehicle are used:
small vehicles which can carry 5 people and 600 kg of baggage
large vehicles which can carry 8 people and 300 kg of baggage.
Only 8 small and 7 large vehicles are available.

(a) (i) $x > 1 \cdot 5y = \frac{3}{2} y$

So $y < \frac{2x}{3}$.

(ii) $x > 12$, $y > 5$, $x + y \leqslant 35$.

(b)

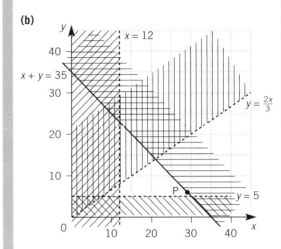

(c) (29, 6) marked on graph.

Cost $= 29 \times 25 + 6 \times 20$

$= 725 + 120$

$= \$845$.

(a) If x small and y large vehicles are used,
(i) explain why $5x + 8y \geqslant 60$.
(ii) Write down three other inequalities, other than $x \geqslant 0$, $y \geqslant 0$, which must be satisfied by x and y.

(b) Represent these inequalities on a graph, shading the unwanted regions.

(c) (i) Mark with dots on the graph all the possible combinations of vehicles.
(ii) What is the smallest number of vehicles possible?
(iii) List the ways this number can be obtained.

4 A photographer charges $10 for an individual photo and $30 for a set of six.
She always sells more individual photos than sets in a week.
She sells x individual photos and y sets of photos in a week.
She needs to earn at least $300 a week.

(a) Write down two inequalities involving x and y, other than $x \geqslant 0$, $y \geqslant 0$.

(b) Represent these inequalities on a graph, shading the unwanted regions.

(c) To produce an individual photo it takes 1 hour and to produce a set is takes 2 hours.
(i) What is the least time she can work and earn at least $300?
(ii) How many individual photos and how many sets does she produce in this time?

Interpreting graphs

Graphs in real situations

To interpret real-life graphs:

- look at the labels on the axes – they tell you what the graph is about
- notice whether the graph is a straight line or a curve
- the slope of the graph gives you the rate of change
- for distance–time graphs the rate of change is the velocity
- for speed–time graphs the rate of change is the acceleration
- the area under a speed–time graph = distance.

Constant rate of change

Rate of change increasing

Rate of change decreasing

No change for the variable on the *y* axis

> Remember to find the rate of change for each part of the graph. If it is zero, say how long this lasts.

Example

Asif walked to the bus stop, waited for the bus, and then travelled on the bus to school. The graph is a distance–time graph for Asif's journey.

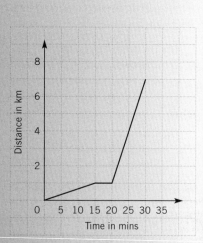

(a) How long did Asif wait at the bus stop?
(b) How far did Asif travel
    (i) on foot **(ii)** by bus?
(c) How fast did Asif walk?
(d) What was the average speed of the bus?
(e) Why are the sections of the graph unlikely, in reality, to be totally straight?

(a) 5 mins
(b) (i) 1 km **(ii)** 6 km
(c) $\frac{1}{15}$ km/min or 4 km/h
(d) $\frac{6}{10}$ km/min or 36 km/h
(e) Stops and starts are likely to be gradual not sudden.

Now try these:

Describe what is really happening for these graphs.

1 (a)

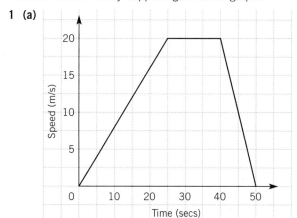

(b)

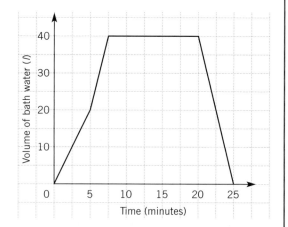

Drawing graphs

- Always label your axes with the quantity and the unit.
- Sometimes only a sketch is asked for, not an accurate plot. Always check whether the rate of change is constant, increasing or decreasing.

Example

Water is poured into this vessel at a constant rate. Sketch a graph of depth of water (*d* cm) against time (*t* secs).

Now try these:

2 A car is travelling at 70 km/h, when it approaches some roadworks where the speed limit is 50 km/h. It slows down from 70 km/h to 50 km/h in 2 mins. It goes through the roadworks at 50 km/h in 5 mins and then accelerates back to 70 km/h in 30 secs.
Draw a velocity–time graph to show this.

3 Find the distance travelled in the first 40 secs in question 1(a).

4 Water is poured into this vessel at a constant rate.
Sketch a graph of depth of water (*d* cm) against time (*t* secs).

Example continued

Since the radius is decreasing at first, the rate of change will increase and then become constant.

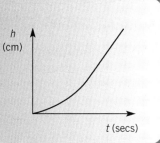

Here is an exam question   ...and its solution

Tom leaves home at 8.20 a.m. and goes to school on a moped. The graph shows his distance from the school in kilometres.

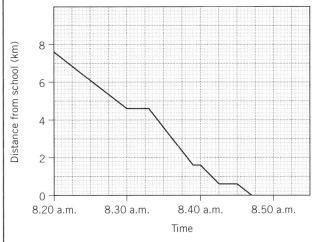

(a) How far does Tom live from school?
(b) Write down the time that Tom arrives at the school.
(c) Tom stopped three times on the journey. For how many minutes was he at the last stop?
(d) Calculate his speed in km/h between 8.20 a.m. and 8.30 a.m.

(a) 7·6km
(b) 8.47 a.m.
(c) 2·5 minutes
(d) Distance = 7·6 − 4·6 = 3 km
Time = 10 mins
Speed = $\frac{3}{10} \times 60$ = 18 km/h

Now try these exam questions:

1 Steve travelled from home to school by walking to a bus stop and then catching a school bus.
  (a) Use the information below to construct a distance–time graph for Steve's journey.
    Steve left home at 08.00.
    He walked at 6 km/h for 10 minutes.
    He then waited for 5 minutes before catching the bus.
    The bus took him a further 8 km to school at a steady speed of 32 km/h.
  (b) How far was Steve from home at 08.20?

2 The graph below describes a real-life situation. Describe a possible situation that is occurring.

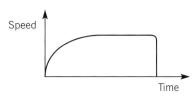

3 The diagrams show the cross-sections of three swimming pools. Water is pumped into all three at a constant rate. Sketch graphs of depth against time for each.

    (a)   (b)   (c)

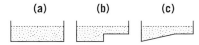

Quadratic and other functions

Quadratic graphs

- Graphs of equations $y = ax^2 + bx + c$ are parabolas. Their shape is

 or

For $a > 0$ For $a < 0$.

When drawing an accurate graph, use a table to work out the points, even if you are not asked to do so.

As well as doing it by hand, you can also use a spreadsheet to work out the values and draw these graphs.

- All parabolas are symmetrical. This symmetry can be seen on the graph and can often be seen in the table as well.

Now try these:

1 (a) Complete this table for $y = x^2 - 3x + 4$.

x	⁻1	0	1	2	3	4
y						

(b) Explain why it is a good idea to add an extra column to the table and work out the value of y when $x = 1·5$.

(c) Draw the graph for ⁻1 ≤ x ≤ 4.

Example

Complete this table for $y = x^2 - 4x + 3$ and draw the graph for –1 ≤ x ≤ 5.

x	⁻1	0	1	2	3	4	5
y	8	3	0	⁻1	0	3	8

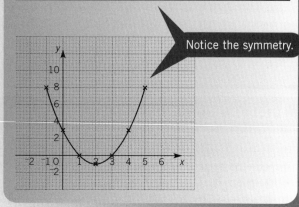

Notice the symmetry.

2 Complete this table and draw the graph for $y = 2x^2 - 5x$ for ⁻2 ≤ x ≤ 5.

x	⁻2	⁻1	0	1	2	3	4	5
y								

Using graphs to solve quadratic equations

- The solution of $ax^2 + bx + c = k$ is the values of x where the graph of $y = ax^2 + bx + c$ crosses the line $y = k$.
- The solution of the simultaneous equations $y = ax^2 + bx + c$ and $y = mx + k$ is the values of x where the two graphs cross.

Now try these:

3 Use the graph you drew in question 1 to solve the following equations.
  (a) $x^2 - 3x + 4 = 4$
  (b) $x^2 - 3x + 4 = 7$
  (c) $x^2 - 3x + 4 = x + 2$

4 Use the graph you drew in question 2 to solve the following equations.
  (a) $2x^2 - 5x = 0$
  (b) $2x^2 - 5x = ⁻1$
  (c) $2x^2 - 7x = 1$

5 Solve graphically, drawing the graphs for values of x from ⁻1 to 3, the simultaneous equations below.
  $y = x^2 - 2x + 1$ $y = 2 - x$

Example

Use the graph of $y = x^2 - 4x + 3$ (drawn above) to solve the following equations.
(a) $x^2 - 4x + 3 = 0$ (c) $x^2 - 4x + 3 = x$
(b) $x^2 - 4x + 3 = 6$ (d) $x^2 - 2x - 2 = 0$

(a) Look at where the graph crosses $y = 0$, the x-axis, the solution is $x = 1$ or 3.
(b) Look at where the graph crosses the line $y = 6$, the solution is $x = ⁻0·6$ or 4·6, to 1 d.p.
(c) This is where the graph crosses the line $y = x$. When this line is added to the graph it can be seen that the solution is $x = 0·7$ or 4·3, to 1 d.p.
(d) Manipulating $x^2 - 2x - 2 = 0$ to give $x^2 - 4x + 3$ on the left-hand side gives $x^2 - 4x + 3 = 5 - 2x$.
So the line to draw is $y = 5 - 2x$. When this line is added to the graph it can be seen that the solution is $x = 2·7$ or ⁻0·7, to 1 d.p.

Cubic, reciprocal and exponential graphs

You also need to be able to recognise the shape of cubic, reciprocal and exponential graphs, and to draw these graphs.

- The cubic graph $y = ax^3$ has this shape when $a > 0$, and is reflected in the x-axis when $a < 0$.

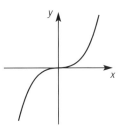

- The reciprocal graph $y = \dfrac{a}{x}$ has this shape when $a > 0$, and is reflected in the x-axis when $a < 0$.

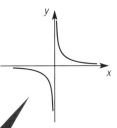

In this example the shape of the 'double bend' is more pronounced than in the graph of $y = ax^3$. This is due to the extra term $^-3x^2$ in the equation.

The graph is in two separate curves. You cannot use 0 as a value for x, since you cannot divide a number by 0.

- The exponential graph $y = k^x$, for $k > 1$ has this shape.

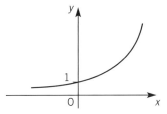

- You will only be asked to work out the values for integer values of x.

- All exponential graphs go through the point $(0, 1)$ since $k^0 = 1$ for all positive values of k. When $k > 1$, they increase steeply for $x > 0$, and are small when x is negative. This is reversed for $0 < k < 1$.

Example

Draw the graph of $y = x^3 - 3x^2$ for values of x from $^-1$ to 4.

Use your graph to solve the equation $x^3 - 3x^2 = ^-1$.

Make a table for the values:

x	$^-2$	$^-1$	0	1	2	3	4
y	$^-20$	$^-4$	0	$^-2$	$^-4$	0	16

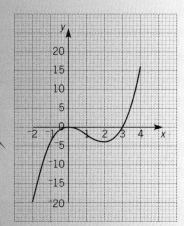

The solution of the equation is where the curve crosses the line $y = ^-1$. The solution is $x = ^-0.5, 0.7$ or 2.9.

Example

Draw $y = 3^x$ and $y = \left(\dfrac{1}{2}\right)^x$ on the same grid.

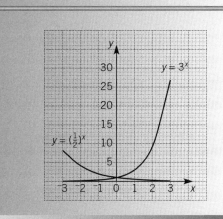

Now try these:

6 Draw the graph of $y = \dfrac{12}{x}$ for values of x from $^-12$ to 12. Use the same scale on both axes.

7 Draw the graph of $y = x^3 - 2x$ for values of x from $^-2$ to 2. Use your graph to find the roots of the equation $x^3 - 2x = 0$ to 1 d.p. Then use trial and improvement to find the positive root correct to 2 d.p.

8 Draw the graph of $y = 2^x$ for values of x from $^-1$ to 4.
Use your graph to find, to 1 d.p., the value of x for which $2^x = 10$.

To find the equation of the required line take $2x^3 - 5x^2 - 1$ and manipulate it to get $\frac{1}{x^2}$.

$$2x^3 - 5x^2 - 1 = 0 \quad \text{add 1 to both sides}$$
$$2x^3 - 5x^2 = 1 \quad \text{factorise left-hand side}$$
$$x^2(2x - 5) = 1 \quad \text{divide both sides by } x^2$$
$$2x - 5 = \frac{1}{x^2}$$

The equaton of the required line is $y = 2x - 5$

Plot the curve $y = \frac{1}{x^2}$ and the line $y = 2x - 5$.

Read off the x values where the curve and the line intersect.

Example

Plot the graph of $y = \frac{1}{x^2}$ for $^-3 \leqslant x \leqslant 3$.

By drawing a suitable line, use your graph to solve the equation $2x^3 - 5x^2 - 1 = 0$.

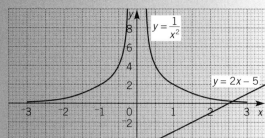

The solution of the equation $2x^3 - 5x^2 - 1 = 0$ from the graph is $x = 2 \cdot 6$.

Now try these:

9 Draw the graph of $y = x^2 - 3x + 5$ for $^-4 \leqslant x \leqslant 5$.
Using the graph, and by drawing suitable lines, solve the following equations.

(a) $x^2 - 3x + 5 = 4$ (b) $x^2 - 4x + 2 = 0$ (c) $x^2 - 5x = 0$

10 Draw the graph of $y = \frac{1}{x}$ for $^-5 \leqslant x \leqslant 5$.
Use your graph to solve the following equations.

(a) $\frac{1}{x} = 3x + 1$ (b) $x^2 - 2x - 1 = 0$

11 Draw the graph of $y = \frac{1}{x^2}$ for $^-3 \leqslant x \leqslant 3$.
Use your graph to solve the equation $x^3 + 2x^2 - 1 = 0$.

Here is an exam question   ...and its solution

In this question, part of the graph was drawn. This helped not only with drawing the graph but also with some of the answers for parts **(c)** and **(d)**.

(a) Complete the table below for $y = x^3 - 2x^2 + 1$.

x	$^-1$	$^-0 \cdot 5$	0
y		0·375	

(b) Part of the graph is drawn on the grid. Add the three points from the table and complete the curve.

(c) Use the graph to solve the equation
$x^3 - 2x^2 + 1 = 0$.

(d) By drawing a suitable straight line on the graph, solve the equation $x^3 - 2x^2 - x + 1 = 0$.

(a)

x	$^-1$	$^-0 \cdot 5$	0
y	$^-2$	0·375	1

(b)

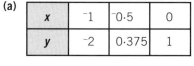

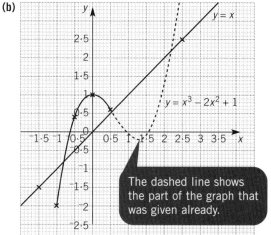

The dashed line shows the part of the graph that was given already.

The solution is where the graph crosses the line $y = 0$.

(c) $x = {}^-0 \cdot 6$, 1 or 1·6.

(d) Manipulating the equation gives $x^3 - 2x^2 + 1 = x$.
So the line to draw is $y = x$. The solution is
$x = {}^-0 \cdot 8$, 0·6 or 2·2.

Now try these exam questions:

1 **(a)** Complete the table for $y = 4x - x^2$ and draw the graph.

x	$^-1$	0	1	2	3	4	5
y			3			0	

(b) Use your graph to find:

    (i) the value of x when $4x - x^2$ is as large as possible

    (ii) between which values of x the value of $4x - x^2 - 2$ is larger than 0.

2 The diagram shows the graphs P, Q, R, S, T and U.
State which of these graphs could correspond to each of the following equations.

(a) $y = x^3 - 1$ **(b)** $y = x^2 - 1$ **(c)** $y = x - 1$

P
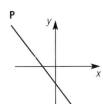

Q
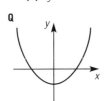

R
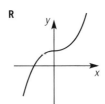

S
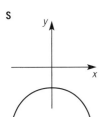

T
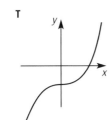

U
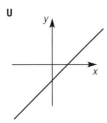

3 The volume, V cm^3, of this cuboid is given by $V = x^3 + 6x^2$.

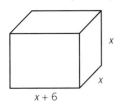

(a) Draw the graph of $V = x^3 + 6x^2$ for values of x from 1 to 6.

x	1	2	3	4	5	6
V						

(b) Use your graph to find the dimensions of the cuboid if its volume is 200 cm^3.

4 **(a)** Draw the graph of $y = \frac{2}{x}$ for values of x from $^-5$ to 5.

(b) Use your graph to solve the equation $\frac{2}{x} = 0.8$.

5 **(a)** Complete the table of values and draw the graph of $y = x^3 - 4x - 1$ for values of x from $^-3$ to 3.

x	$^-3$	$^-2$	$^-1$	0	1	2	3
y	$^-16$		2	$^-1$	$^-4$	$^-1$	14

(b) Use your graph to solve the equation $x^3 - 4x - 1 = 0$.

(c) By drawing a suitable straight line on your graph, solve the equation $x^3 - 6x - 3 = 0$.

6 Draw the graph of $y = x^3$ for $^-2 \le x \le 2$.
Use your graph to solve the equation $x^3 - 2x - 1 = 0$.

7 Draw the graph of $y = \frac{2}{x^2} - x$ for $^-4 \le x \le 3$.
Use your graph to solve the equation $2x^3 + 7x^2 - 6 = 0$.

Graphs – gradient and area

Gradient

- Gradient = $\dfrac{\text{increase in } y}{\text{increase in } x}$.
- The gradient of a curve varies at different points on the curve.
- To find the gradient of a curve at a given point, first draw a tangent to the curve at that point.
- Then find the gradient of the tangent.
- The gradient of the curve is the same as the gradient of the tangent, but because of inaccuracies of drawing can only be regarded as an estimate.

> Remember a line that goes 'downhill' from left to right has a negative gradient.

> When choosing two points on a tangent to find the gradient, make the x increase an easy number.

Example

Find the gradient of the curve $y = x^2$ at the point (2, 4).

Plot the graph and draw a tangent to the curve at (2, 4).

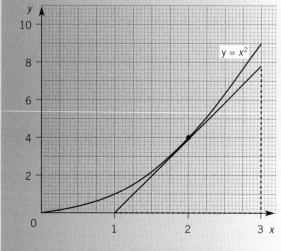

Gradient $= \dfrac{7{\cdot}8 - 0}{3 - 1} = \dfrac{7{\cdot}8}{2} = 3{\cdot}9.$

Now try these:

1 Draw a graph of $y = x^3$ for $0 \leqslant x \leqslant 3$.
Estimate the gradient at
(a) (1, 1)   (b) (2, 8).

2 Draw a graph of $y = \dfrac{12}{x}$ for $^-12 \leqslant x \leqslant 12$.

Estimate the gradient at
(a) $x = 2$ (b) $x = 4$ (c) $x = {}^-4$.

3 Draw a graph of $y = x^2 - 3x$ for $^-2 \leqslant x \leqslant 5$.
Estimate the gradient at
(a) $x = {}^-1$ (b) $x = 2$.

4 Draw a graph of $y = x^3 - 2x$ for $^-3 \leqslant x \leqslant 3$.
Estimate the gradient at
(a) $x = {}^-2$ (b) $x = 0$ (c) $x = 2$.

Rates of change

- When the graph is a practical graph the gradient is called a rate of change and has units.
- The gradient of a distance–time graph represents speed (usual units ms⁻¹).
- The gradient of a speed–time graph represents acceleration (usual units ms⁻²)

> Remember, when reading off y increases and x increases, use the scales; do not count squares.

Example

The graph shows the area (A cm²) of an ink blot against time (t secs).
Find the rate of change when $t = 4$.

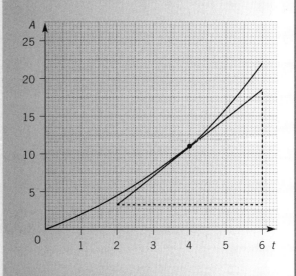

Draw a tangent to the curve at $t = 4$.

Rate of change $= \dfrac{18 \cdot 5 - 3 \cdot 5}{6 - 2} = \dfrac{15}{4} = 3 \cdot 75$ cm²/s.

Now try these:

5 The graph shows distance (d m) against time (t secs).
Estimate the speed at
(a) $t = 2$ **(b)** $t = 4$.

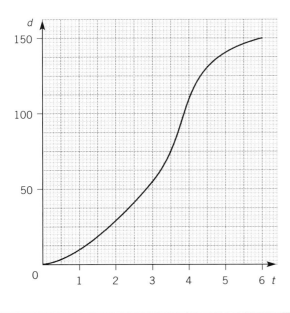

6 The graph shows speed (v ms⁻¹) against time (t secs).
Estimate the acceleration at
(a) $t = 2$ **(b)** $t = 8$.

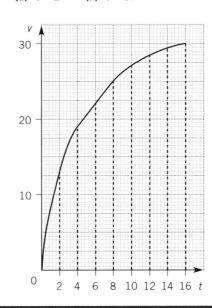

Area under a graph

- To find the area under staight-line graphs, use the formulae for areas of a triangle, rectangle and trapezium.
- For the area under a curve you need to estimate by counting squares or by dividing up the area into strips and approximating with trapezia.
- The area under a speed–time graph represents distance.

> Area of trapezium = $\frac{1}{2} \times (a + b) \times$ width.

Example

Estimate the distance travelled in the 16 seconds in question 6.

Split up the area into strips of width 2 seconds and assume the tops are straight.

Strip 1	$\frac{1}{2} \times 13 \times 2$	$= 13$
Strip 2	$\frac{1}{2} \times (13 + 19) \times 2$	$= 32$
Strip 3	$\frac{1}{2} \times (19 + 22) \times 2$	$= 41$
Strip 4	$\frac{1}{2} \times (22 + 25) \times 2$	$= 47$
Strip 5	$\frac{1}{2} \times (25 + 27) \times 2$	$= 52$
Strip 6	$\frac{1}{2} \times (27 + 28.5) \times 2$	$= 55.5$
Strip 7	$\frac{1}{2} \times (28.5 + 29.5) \times 2$	$= 58$
Strip 8	$\frac{1}{2} \times (29.5 + 30) \times 2$	$= 59.5$
Total		**358 m**

Now try these:

7 Draw a graph of $y = 5x - x^2$ for $0 \leqslant x \leqslant 5$.
Estimate the area between the curve and the x-axis.

8 Draw a graph of $x^3 - 2x + 5$ for $0 \leqslant x \leqslant 3$.
Estimate the area between the curve, the x-axis, the y-axis and the line $x = 3$.

9 Draw a graph of $y = x^2 - 6x + 10$ for $0 \leqslant x \leqslant 6$.
On the same graph draw the line $y = 5$.
Estimate the area between the curve and the line.

10 The graph shows the speed of a bicycle (v ms^{-1}) against time (t secs).
Estimate the distance travelled in the first 7 seconds.

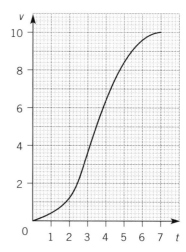

Algebra

Here is an exam question   ...and its solution

The rate at which a hospital uses gas between 6 a.m. and 8 a.m. is shown in the graph

(a) Estimate the area beneath the curve.
(b) What does the area found in part (a) represent? Specify its units.

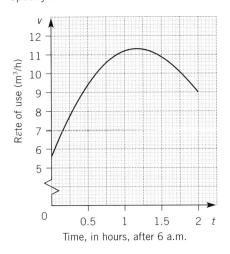

(a) Using strips of width 0·5 hours:

$$\frac{1}{2}(5\cdot6 + 9\cdot4) \times 0\cdot5 \quad = \quad 3\cdot75$$

$$\frac{1}{2}(9\cdot4 + 11\cdot2) \times 0\cdot5 \quad = \quad 5\cdot15$$

$$\frac{1}{2}(11\cdot2 + 10\cdot8) \times 0\cdot5 = \quad 5\cdot5$$

$$\frac{1}{2}(10\cdot8 + 9) \times 0\cdot5 \quad = \quad 4\cdot95$$

Total   19·35

> Remember to use the scale to find the heights of the trapezia.

Area under curve is approximately 19·4 or 19.

(b) The total volume of gas used by the hospital in the 2 hours. The units are cubic metres (m^3).

Now try these exam questions:

1 Ameni is cycling at 4 metres per second.
After 3·5 seconds she starts to decelerate and after a further 2·5 seconds she stops.
The diagram shows the speed–time graph of her journey.
Calculate
(a) the acceleration between $t = 3\cdot5$ and $t = 6$
(b) the distance travelled during the 6 seconds.

2 The number of bacteria in a colony multiplies by a factor of 3 every hour.
Initially there are 20 bacteria.
(a) Copy and complete the table

Time (t hours)	0	1	2	3	4	5
Number of bacteria (n)	20	60				

(b) Write down the formula for the number of bacteria, n, after t hours.
(c) Draw a graph showing how the number of bacteria changes in the 5 hours.
(d) (i) By drawing a tangent to the curve in part (c), calculate the gradient of the curve at the point where $t = 3\cdot5$.
  (ii) What information does this gradient represent?

3 Dimitra stands by a river and watches a fish. The distance (d metres) of the fish from Dimitra, after t minutes, is given by

$$d = (t + 1)^2 + \frac{48}{t + 1} - 20.$$

Some values of d and t are given in the table below.

t	0	0·5	1	1·5	2	2·5	3	3·5	4	5	6	7
d	p	14·3	8	5·5	5	6	8	10·9	14·6	q	35·9	r

(a) Find the values of p, q and r.
(b) Draw the graph of $d = (t + 1)^2 + \frac{48}{t + 1} - 20$ for $0 \leqslant t \leqslant 7$.

(c) Mark and label the point F on your graph where the fish is 12 metres from Dimitra and swimming **away** from her.

Write down the value of t at this point, correct to 1 d.p.

(d) For how many seconds is the fish less than 10 metres from Dimitra?

(e) By drawing a suitable line on your graph, calculate the speed of the fish when $t = 2 \cdot 5$.

4 The graph represents the motion of a car.

v is the speed in ms^{-1} and t is the time in seconds.

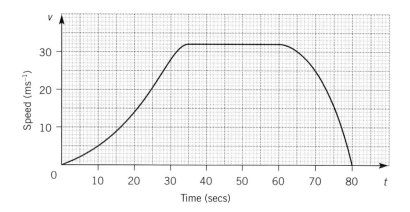

(a) Use the graph to estimate the acceleration of the car when $t = 30$.

State the units of your answer.

(b) Estimate the distance the car travelled in the 80 seconds.

5 A family took a holiday on a boat.

The graph shows the speed of the boat in km/h plotted against the time for the first three hours of the journey.

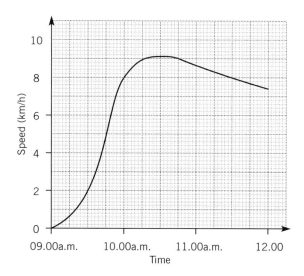

(a) Estimate the distance the family travelled during this time.

(b) Write down the time when the acceleration of the boat was greatest.

Functions

Notation

f: $x \rightarrow 3x + 2$ means f is the function that maps x onto $3x + 2$.

It is more commonly written as:

$f(x) = 3x + 2$.

This is read as f of x equals $3x + 2$.

Using functions

- f(7) means the value of the function when $x = 7$.
- To find the value of a function, substitute the number or expression in the brackets for x in the formula.

Example

For the function $f(x) = 3x + 2$, find

(a) f (7)   **(b)** $f\left(\frac{1}{2}\right)$ **(c)** f (2x).

(a) $f(7) = 3 \times 7 + 2 = 23$

(b) $f\left(\frac{1}{2}\right) = 3 \times \frac{1}{2} + 2 = 3\frac{1}{2}$

(c) $f(2x) = 3 \times (2x) + 2 = 6x + 2$

- When you are given the value of the function and want to find the value of x, put the formula for the function equal to the number or expression. Then solve the equation to find the value of x.

Example

For the function $g(x) = 2x - 1$, find the value of x for which

(a) g(x) = 11   **(b)** g(x) = x + 7.

(a) $g(x) = 11$
   $2x - 1 = 11$
   $2x = 12$
   $x = 6$

(b) $g(x) = x + 7$
   $2x - 1 = x + 7$
   $2x - x = 7 + 1$
   $x = 8$

Now try these:

1 For the funcion $f(x) = 5x + 1$, find
   (a) f(7)   **(b)** f(¯3)   **(c)** f(0).

2 For the function $g(x) = 3 - 4x$, find
   (a) g(6)   **(b)** $g\left(1\frac{1}{2}\right)$ **(c)** g(2x).

3 For the function $h(x) = 3(2x - 7)$, find
   (a) h(5)   **(b)** h(3x)   **(c)** h(x − 1).

4 For the function $p(x) = \frac{2}{1-x}$, find
   (a) p(0)   **(b)** p(¯4)   **(c)** $p\left(\frac{1}{2}\right)$.

5 For the function $q(x) = 3x^2 - 2$, find
   (a) q(5)   **(c)** q(2x)   **(e)** q(2x) + 5.
   (b) q(¯1)   **(d)** q(x + 3)

6 For the functions $f(x) = 5x - 4$ and $g(x) = 7x + 2$, find x for which
   (a) f(x) = 6   **(c)** f(x) = g(x)
   (b) g(x) = ¯12   **(d)** 3f(x) = 2g(x).

Composite functions

- When two or more functions are combined, the result is called a composite function.
- The composite of the two functions f(x) and g(x) is written fg(x) or f[g(x)].
- In general, the composite fg(x) is *not* the same as gf(x).
- To find the value of a composite function fg(x), find the value of g(x) first, then put the answer in place of x in the formula for f(x).

Find g(3) first.

Then put the answer in place of x in the formula for f(x).

Replace x in the formula for f(x) with the formula for g(x).

Replace *every* x in the formula for g(x) with the formula for f(x)

Example

For $f(x) = 3x + 2$ and $g(x) = x^2 - 2x + 1$,

(a) find
   (i) fg(3)   **(ii)** gf(0)

(b) find the formula for
   (i) fg(x)   **(ii)** gf(x).

(a) (i) $fg(3) = f[g(3)]$
$= f[3^2 - 2 \times 3 + 1]$
$= f[4]$
$= 3 \times 4 + 2$
$= 14$

(ii) $gf(0) = g[f(0)]$
$= g[3 \times 0 + 2]$
$= g[2]$
$= 2^2 - 2 \times 2 + 1$
$= 1$

(b) (i) $fg(x) = f[g(x)]$
$= f[x^2 - 2x + 1]$
$= 3(x^2 - 2x + 1) + 2$
$= 3x^2 - 6x + 5$

(ii) $gf(x) = g[f(x)]$
$= g[3x + 2]$
$= (3x + 2)^2 - 2(3x + 2) + 1$
$= (9x^2 + 12x + 4) - 6x - 4 + 1$
$= 9x^2 + 6x + 1$

Now try these:

7 For $f(x) = x - 3$ and $g(x) = x + 1$, find
   (a) fg(3)
   (b) gf(⁻3)
   (c) a formula for
      (i) fg(x)   **(ii)** gf(x).

8 For $h(x) = 5x + 7$ and $k(x) = 2x - 4$, find
   (a) kh(4)
   (b) hk$\left(\frac{-1}{2}\right)$
   (c) a formula for
      (i) kh(x)   **(ii)** hk(x).

9 For $p(x) = 4x + 7$ and $q(x) = \frac{x + 3}{2}$, find
   (a) pq(5)
   (b) qp$\left(\frac{1}{2}\right)$
   (c) a formula for
      (i) pq(x)   **(ii)** qp(x).

10 For $f(x) = 1 - 3x$ and $g(x) = 2(x + 4)$ find
   (a) fg(0)
   (b) gf(⁻2)
   (c) a formula for
      (i) fg(x)   **(ii)** gf(x).

11 For $h(x) = 4x - 3$ and $j(x) = x^2$ find a formula for
   (a) hj(x)   **(b)** jh(x).

12 For $f(x) = 1 + 2x$ and $g(x) = x^2 - 2x + 1$ find a formula for
   (a) fg(x)   **(b)** gf(x).

Inverse functions

- An inverse function has exactly the opposite effect as a given function.
- For the function $f(x)$ the inverse is written $f^{-1}(x)$ so that when $f(x) = x + 1$, $f^{-1}(x) = x - 1$.
- To find the formula of an inverse function, put y in place of $f(x)$.
  Rearrange the formula to make x the subject.
  Replacing y with x gives the formula of the inverse function.

Now try these:

13 For $f(x) = 7x + 2$, find

   (a) $f^{-1}(x)$ **(b)** $f^{-1}(2)$ **(c)** $f^{-1}(0)$.

14 For $g(x) = \frac{x}{4} - 1$, find

   (a) $g^{-1}(x)$ **(b)** $g^{-1}\left(1\frac{1}{4}\right)$ **(c)** $g^{-1}(^-5)$.

15 Find the inverse of each of the following functions.

   (a) $p(x) = 3(x + 2)$ **(c)** $k(x) = 4(3x - 6)$

   (b) $h(x) = \frac{2x - 5}{4}$ **(d)** $t(x) = 5x^2 + 3$

Example

For $t(x) = 5x - 4$, find

(a) a formula for $t^{-1}(x)$

(b) (i) $t^{-1}(1)$ **(ii)** $t^{-1}(^-3)$.

(a)
$$t(x) = 5x - 4$$
$$y = 5x - 4$$
$$5x = y + 4$$
$$x = \frac{y + 4}{5} \quad \text{so} \quad t^{-1}(x) = \frac{x + 4}{5}$$

(b) (i) $t^{-1}(1) = \frac{1 + 4}{5} = 1$

   (ii) $t^{-1}(^-3) = \frac{^-3 + 4}{5} = \frac{1}{5}$

Alternative method for **(b)** without finding $t^{-1}(x)$.

(b) (i)
$$1 = 5x - 4$$
$$x = 1 \quad \text{so} \quad t^{-1}(1) = 1$$

   (ii)
$$^-3 = 5x - 4$$
$$x = \frac{1}{5} \quad \text{so} \quad t^{-1}(^-3) = \frac{1}{5}$$

Here is an exam question   ...and its solution

For the function $f(x) = px + q$, $f(5) = 7$ and $f(1) = 3$.
Find the values of p and q.

> You are given the value of the function for two values of x so you can form a pair of simultaneous equations.

$f(5) = p \times 5 + q$ so $5p + q = 7$.

$f(1) = p \times 1 + q$ so $p + q = 3$.

Subtract the simultaneous equations
$$4p = 4$$
$$p = 1.$$
Substitute the value of p
$$1 + q = 3$$
$$q = 2.$$

Now try these exam questions:

1 $f : x \rightarrow 2x - 1$ and $g : x \rightarrow x^2 - 1$.

   Find, in their simplest form,

   (a) $f^{-1}(x)$ **(b)** $gf(x)$.

2 $f(x) = x^{\frac{1}{3}}$ and $g(x) = 2x^2 - 5$.

   (a) Find **(i)** $g(4)$ **(ii)** $fg(4)$.

   (b) Find expressions for

       (i) $gf(x)$ **(ii)** $f^{-1}(x)$.

3 $f : x \rightarrow 3x - 5$ and $g : x \rightarrow x + 1$

   (a) Calculate $f(^-1)$.

   (b) Find $f^{-1}(x)$.

   (c) Find $fg(x)$. Give your answer in its simplest form.

   (d) Solve the equation $3f(x) = 5g(x)$.

4 $f(x) = \frac{1}{3}(2x + 5)$

   (a) Find $f(^-4)$.   **(b)** Find $f^{-1}(x)$.

5 $f(x) = 3x + 1$ and $g(x) = 2x^2$.

   Find, in their simplest form,

   (a) $f^{-1}(x)$ **(c)** $gf(x)$

   (b) $fg(2)$ **(d)** $ff(x)$.

6 $f(x) = 2x + 1$ and $g(x) = \frac{x}{3} - 5$

   (a) Find $f(^-1)$.

   (b) Find $f^{-1}(x)$.

   (c) Find $g^{-1}(x)$.

   (d) Find $fg(0)$.

   (e) Find $fg(x)$ in its simplest form.

Sets and Venn diagrams

One set

- Sets are a way of classifying groups of objects and the relationships between them.
- Sets are written out using curly brackets, with commas between each item or element of the set. Or they are described after using a symbol and a colon(:).
- 3 ∈ S means that 3 is in set S.
- yellow ∉ S means that yellow is not in set S.
- The number of elements in set S is written n(S).
- The symbol ∅ is used for a set which is empty.
- The symbol ℰ is used for the entire or **universal** set of objects being considered.
- S' is the set of everything in ℰ which is not in set S. It is called the complement of set S.
- Venn diagrams show sets in a diagram instead of using symbols.
- A Venn diagram shows the universal set as a rectangle, with other sets inside as ovals or circles.

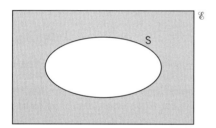

In this Venn diagram, the shaded area represents S'.

Example

The set A of integers from 2 to 6 inclusive is {2, 3, 4, 5, 6} or
{x: x is an integer and $1 \leqslant x \leqslant 6$}.

In the example above, $4 \in A$, $8 \notin A$.

In the example above, n(A) = 5.

If ℰ = {1, 2, 3, 4, 5, 6, 7, 8, 9, 10} and set A is as above, A' = {1, 7, 8, 9, 10}.

This Venn diagram shows all the elements of ℰ and whether they are in A or A'.

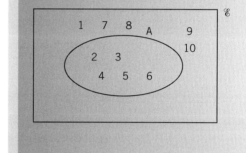

Now try these:

1 List the elements of the set {x: $10 \leqslant x \leqslant 20$ and x is an even integer}.

2 Show that $(4, 1) \in \{(x, y): y = 2x - 7\}$.

3 Draw a Venn diagram to illustrate ℰ = {colours of the rainbow} and S = {red, indigo, violet}.

4 This Venn diagram shows ℰ and A.
   (a) List set A'.
   (b) Write the correct symbol, ∈ or ∉ between each of the following.
      (i) 3   A   (ii) 7   A   (iii) 4   A'

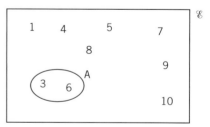

Two or more sets

- The **union** of sets A and B, written A ∪ B is the set of objects belonging to set A or set B or both. It is shown shaded on this Venn diagram.

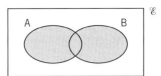

- The **intersection** of sets A and B, written A ∩ B, is the set of objects belonging to both sets A and B. It is shown shaded on this Venn diagram.

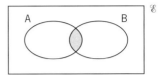

- In this Venn diagram, the sets A and B are **disjoint** and the intersection of A and B is the empty set, written A ∩ B = ∅ or A ∩ B = { }

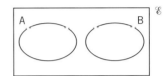

- In this Venn diagram, everything in B is in A. B is a **subset** of A, written B ⊂ A, or as B ⊆ A if B can be A itself.
  When B is a subset of A, A ∪ B = A and A ∩ B = B.

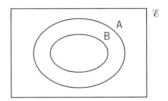

- Venn diagrams can show the numbers of elements in each set, instead of the elements themselves. This can be used to solve set problems.

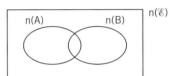

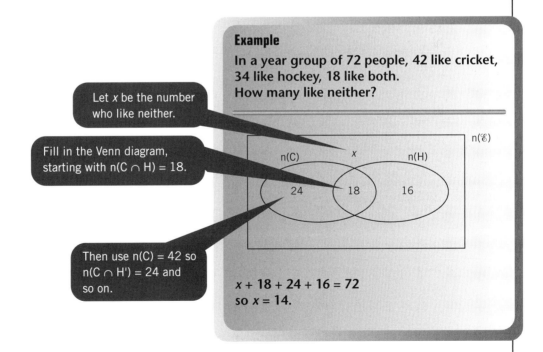

Example

In a year group of 72 people, 42 like cricket, 34 like hockey, 18 like both.
How many like neither?

Let x be the number who like neither.

Fill in the Venn diagram, starting with n(C ∩ H) = 18.

Then use n(C) = 42 so n(C ∩ H') = 24 and so on.

$x + 18 + 24 + 16 = 72$
so $x = 14$.

Now try these:

5 The Venn diagram shows the elements of sets A, B and C. List the elements of these sets.
(a) A ∩ C   (c) B ∪ C
(b) B ∩ C   (d) A ∩ C'

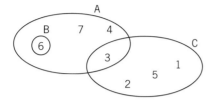

6 List the elements of all the possible subsets of A when A = {a, b, c}.

7 Draw a Venn diagram to show sets A, B and ℰ. Shade the region which represents A ∩ B'.

Here is an exam question   ...and its solution

(a) On this Venn diagram, shade the region which represents (A ∪ B) ∩ C'.

(a)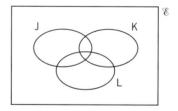

(b) Use set language to describe the region which is shaded on this Venn diagram.

(b) There are two acceptable answers.
(A ∩ B)' or A' ∪ B'.

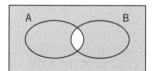

Now try these exam questions:

1 Three sets A, B and C are such that A ⊂ C, B ⊂ C and A ∩ B ≠ ∅.
Draw a Venn diagram to show this information.

2 ℰ = {x: x is an integer and 1 ⩽ x ⩽ 12},
P = {x: x is an even integer} and Q = {3, 6, 9, 12}.
List the elements of
(a) P ∩ Q   (b) (P ∪ Q)'.

3 In a class of students, 11 play a stringed instrument, 15 play a wind instrument, 6 play both and 10 play neither.
Draw a Venn diagram to show this information and find the total number of students in the class.

4 (a)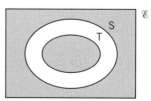

On a copy of this Venn diagram, shade the set J ∩ (K ∪ L).

(b) Express in set notation, as simply as possible, the set shaded in this Venn diagram.

(c) In a class of 32 students, 12 study chemistry and 18 study French. 9 students in the class study neither of these.
Using a Venn diagram, or otherwise, find how many students study chemistry but not French.

Matrices

Order

- The size or **order** of a matrix is established by looking first at the number of rows and second at the number of columns. The order is written as $m \times n$ where m is the number of rows and n is the number of columns.

Now try these:

1 Write down the order of these matrices

   (a) $A = \begin{pmatrix} 7 & 1 & 2 & 4 \\ 2 & 5 & 3 & 8 \end{pmatrix}$ **(c)** $C = \begin{pmatrix} 3 & 8 & 5 & ^-2 \\ 1 & ^-3 & 2 & 5 \\ 6 & ^-2 & 1 & 4 \end{pmatrix}$

   (b) $B = \begin{pmatrix} 5 & ^-3 \\ ? & 4 \\ ^-1 & 5 \\ 3 & 8 \end{pmatrix}$

2 A shop sells 5 rings, 8 bracelets and 10 necklaces one week and 11 rings, 6 bracelets and 9 necklaces the next week. Show this information in a 2×3 matrix.

3 In 2001 a school had 86 students studying Spanish, 58 studying German and 102 studying English. In 2002 the numbers were 92 studying Spanish, 59 studyng German and 98 studying English and in 2003 they were 95 studying Spanish, 56 studying German and 116 studying English. Show this information in a 3×3 matrix.

4 One month a shop sells 3 kg of tea, 8 kg of rice and 2 kg of salt in week 1, 2 kg of tea, 10 kg of rice and 1 kg of salt in week 2, 4 kg of tea, 11 kg of rice and 2 kg of salt in week 3 and 2 kg of tea, 9 kg of rice and 3 kg of salt in week 4. Show this information in a 4×3 matrix.

Example
Write down the order of these matrices.

(a) $A = \begin{pmatrix} 2 & 5 & 3 \\ 4 & 2 & 5 \end{pmatrix}$ **(c)** $C = \begin{pmatrix} 5 \\ ^-3 \\ 4 \end{pmatrix}$

(b) $B = \begin{pmatrix} 2 & 1 & 3 & 3 \\ 4 & 1 & 2 & 3 \\ 5 & 2 & 2 & 1 \end{pmatrix}$

(a) 2×3 **(b)** 3×4 **(c)** 3×1

> The first figure is the number of *rows*, the second is the number of *columns*.

Example
A small bakery makes 45 white, 30 wholemeal and 20 granary loaves on Friday. On Saturday it makes 40 white, 20 wholemeal and 15 granary loaves. Show this information in a 3×2 matrix.

$\begin{pmatrix} 45 & 40 \\ 30 & 20 \\ 20 & 15 \end{pmatrix}$ The matrix must have three rows and two columns

Adding and subtracting

- Matrices can only be added or subtracted if they are of the same order.
- To add, or subtract, matrices it is necessary to combine elements that occupy corresponding positions.

> $5 + 3 = 8$

Example
Work out the following.

(a) $\begin{pmatrix} 5 & 7 & 3 \\ 2 & 5 & 8 \end{pmatrix} + \begin{pmatrix} 3 & 2 & 6 \\ 5 & 7 & 4 \end{pmatrix}$

(b) $\begin{pmatrix} 26 & 13 \\ 17 & 24 \\ 23 & 15 \end{pmatrix} - \begin{pmatrix} 18 & 11 \\ 23 & 20 \\ 19 & 23 \end{pmatrix}$

(a) $\begin{pmatrix} 8 & 9 & 9 \\ 7 & 12 & 12 \end{pmatrix}$ **(b)** $\begin{pmatrix} 8 & 2 \\ ^-6 & 4 \\ 4 & ^-8 \end{pmatrix}$

Now try these:

5 Write each of the following as a single matrix.

  (a) $\begin{pmatrix} 7 & 3 & 5 & 1 \\ 4 & 5 & 3 & 6 \end{pmatrix} + \begin{pmatrix} 4 & 3 & 2 & 5 \\ 3 & 5 & 7 & 1 \end{pmatrix}$

  (b) $\begin{pmatrix} 24 & 19 \\ ^-8 & 34 \\ 16 & 5 \end{pmatrix} + \begin{pmatrix} 13 & ^-7 \\ 14 & 1 \\ 9 & 31 \end{pmatrix}$

  (c) $\begin{pmatrix} 8 & ^-2 & 3 & 7 \\ 5 & 4 & 2 & 1 \\ ^-2 & 5 & 6 & 4 \end{pmatrix} + \begin{pmatrix} 3 & 6 & 9 & ^-4 \\ 7 & 1 & 5 & 2 \\ 8 & 3 & ^-7 & 4 \end{pmatrix}$

  (d) $\begin{pmatrix} 9 & 5 \\ ^-5 & 2 \end{pmatrix} + \begin{pmatrix} 4 & 7 \\ 3 & 8 \end{pmatrix}$

6 Write each of the following as a single matrix.

  (a) $\begin{pmatrix} 6 & 5 \\ 7 & 4 \end{pmatrix} - \begin{pmatrix} 4 & 7 \\ 8 & 6 \end{pmatrix}$

  (b) $\begin{pmatrix} ^-2 & 5 & 8 \\ 6 & 9 & 1 \\ 3 & 7 & 2 \\ 4 & 1 & 6 \end{pmatrix} - \begin{pmatrix} 5 & 3 & 8 \\ 7 & 2 & 9 \\ 4 & 2 & 5 \\ 3 & 8 & 4 \end{pmatrix}$

  (c) $\begin{pmatrix} 15 & 12 \\ 14 & ^-7 \\ 11 & 9 \end{pmatrix} - \begin{pmatrix} 8 & 5 \\ ^-5 & 18 \\ 9 & 12 \end{pmatrix}$

  (d) $\begin{pmatrix} ^-8 & 6 & 4 & 2 \\ 7 & 5 & ^-3 & 1 \end{pmatrix} - \begin{pmatrix} 5 & 6 & ^-7 & 8 \\ 4 & 5 & 2 & 9 \end{pmatrix}$

Multiplication

- Matrices can be multiplied by a number, known as a *scalar*, or sometimes by another matrix.
- To multiply a matrix by another matrix the number of *columns* in the *first* matrix **must** be the same as the number of *rows* in the *second* matrix.

Example

Work out the following.

(a) $3\begin{pmatrix} 3 & {}^-8 \\ 4 & 5 \end{pmatrix}$ (b) $\frac{1}{2}\begin{pmatrix} 4 & 9 & {}^-2 \\ 3 & 6 & 8 \\ {}^-4 & 1 & {}^-3 \end{pmatrix}$

(a) $\begin{pmatrix} 9 & {}^-24 \\ 12 & 15 \end{pmatrix}$ (b) $\begin{pmatrix} 2 & 4.5 & {}^-1 \\ 1.5 & 3 & 4 \\ {}^-2 & 0.5 & {}^-1.5 \end{pmatrix}$

> *Every* element in the matrix must be multiplied by the scalar

Now try these:

7 Where possible, multiply the matrices.

(a) $\begin{pmatrix} 2 & 3 & 1 \\ 4 & 5 & 3 \end{pmatrix}\begin{pmatrix} 3 & 2 \\ 2 & 4 \\ 1 & 3 \end{pmatrix}$

(b) $\begin{pmatrix} 3 & {}^-2 \\ 1 & 4 \end{pmatrix}\begin{pmatrix} 5 & 2 \\ {}^-3 & 4 \end{pmatrix}$

(c) $\begin{pmatrix} 4 & 2 & 5 \\ 3 & 1 & 3 \end{pmatrix}\begin{pmatrix} 3 & {}^-2 \\ {}^-1 & 4 \end{pmatrix}$

(d) $\begin{pmatrix} 6 & 3 & 2 & {}^-1 \\ 2 & 4 & 0 & 3 \end{pmatrix}\begin{pmatrix} 3 \\ 2 \\ 2 \\ 4 \end{pmatrix}$

(e) $(2 \quad 0 \quad {}^-3)\begin{pmatrix} 2 & 3 \\ 2 & {}^-1 \\ 5 & 4 \end{pmatrix}$

(f) $({}^-3 \quad 2)\begin{pmatrix} 0 & {}^-3 \\ 4 & {}^-2 \end{pmatrix}$

(g) $\begin{pmatrix} 1 & {}^-2 & 3 \\ 3 & 4 & {}^-3 \end{pmatrix}\begin{pmatrix} 2 & {}^-3 & 4 \\ 1 & 0 & 2 \\ 3 & 5 & 2 \end{pmatrix}$

(h) $\begin{pmatrix} 5 & 0 & 2 \\ {}^-3 & 1 & 4 \\ 2 & 6 & 3 \end{pmatrix}\begin{pmatrix} 2 & {}^-3 & 4 \\ 1 & 3 & 5 \\ 0 & 4 & {}^-2 \end{pmatrix}$

Example

Where possible, multiply the matrices.

(a) $\begin{pmatrix} 3 & {}^-8 \\ 4 & 5 \end{pmatrix}\begin{pmatrix} 3 & {}^-8 \\ 4 & 5 \end{pmatrix}$

(b) $\begin{pmatrix} {}^-2 & 4 & 1 \\ 3 & 0 & {}^-5 \end{pmatrix}\begin{pmatrix} 5 & {}^-3 \\ 2 & 1 \\ {}^-4 & 2 \end{pmatrix}$

(c) $\begin{pmatrix} 4 \\ {}^-3 \end{pmatrix}\begin{pmatrix} 3 & {}^-8 \\ 4 & 5 \end{pmatrix}$

(a) $\begin{pmatrix} 3{\times}3 + {}^-8{\times}4 & 3{\times}{}^-8 + {}^-8{\times}5 \\ 4{\times}3 + 5{\times}4 & 4{\times}{}^-8 + 5{\times}5 \end{pmatrix}$

$= \begin{pmatrix} {}^-23 & {}^-64 \\ 32 & {}^-7 \end{pmatrix}$

(b) $\begin{pmatrix} {}^-2{\times}5 + 4{\times}2 + 1{\times}{}^-4 & {}^-2{\times}{}^-3 + 4{\times}1 + 1{\times}2 \\ {}^-2{\times}{}^-3 + 4{\times}1 + 1{\times}2 & 3{\times}{}^-3 + 0{\times}1 + {}^-5{\times}2 \end{pmatrix}$

$= \begin{pmatrix} {}^-6 & 12 \\ 12 & {}^-19 \end{pmatrix}$

(c) Not possible

> There is only one column in the first matrix and there are two rows in the second matrix.

The determinant

The determinant of a 2 × 2 matrix is found by calculating the difference in the products of the leading diagonal and the secondary diagonal.

Example

Find the determinant |**D**| of the matrix

$\mathbf{D} = \begin{pmatrix} 3 & {}^-2 \\ 1 & 4 \end{pmatrix}$.

$|\mathbf{D}| = (3 \times 4) - (1 \times {}^-2)$
$= 12 + 2$
$= 14$

Now try these:

8 Find the determinant of each of these matrices.

(a) $\begin{pmatrix} 5 & 2 \\ 4 & 3 \end{pmatrix}$ (c) $\begin{pmatrix} 8 & 5 \\ 5 & 3 \end{pmatrix}$ (e) $\begin{pmatrix} 4 & {}^-3 \\ 2 & 5 \end{pmatrix}$ (g) $\begin{pmatrix} {}^-4 & {}^-3 \\ 5 & {}^-2 \end{pmatrix}$

(b) $\begin{pmatrix} 3 & 4 \\ 5 & 8 \end{pmatrix}$ (d) $\begin{pmatrix} {}^-3 & 3 \\ 5 & {}^-6 \end{pmatrix}$ (f) $\begin{pmatrix} {}^-3 & 2 \\ {}^-4 & 5 \end{pmatrix}$ (h) $\begin{pmatrix} {}^-6 & {}^-5 \\ {}^-4 & {}^-3 \end{pmatrix}$

The inverse of a matrix

- When two matrices multiply together to give $\begin{pmatrix} 1 & 0 \\ 0 & 1 \end{pmatrix}$, the **identity** matrix, as the outcome then one of the matrices is the inverse of the other.

There are three steps to find an inverse matrix.

Step 1: Reverse the position of the numbers in the leading diagonal.

Step 2: Change the signs of the numbers in the secondary diagonal.

Step 3: Divide all the elements by the determinant.

Now try these:

9 Find the inverse matrix of each of these matrices.

(a) $\begin{pmatrix} 7 & 5 \\ 4 & 3 \end{pmatrix}$

(b) $\begin{pmatrix} 2 & 3 \\ 3 & 5 \end{pmatrix}$

(c) $\begin{pmatrix} 7 & 9 \\ 3 & 4 \end{pmatrix}$

(d) $\begin{pmatrix} ^-8 & 3 \\ 5 & ^-2 \end{pmatrix}$

(e) $\begin{pmatrix} 4 & 2 \\ 8 & 5 \end{pmatrix}$

(f) $\begin{pmatrix} 6 & 4 \\ 5 & 5 \end{pmatrix}$

(g) $\begin{pmatrix} ^-5 & 7 \\ 4 & ^-6 \end{pmatrix}$

(h) $\begin{pmatrix} 6 & 8 \\ 4 & 5 \end{pmatrix}$

Example

Work out the inverse matrix of

(a) **A**, where $A = \begin{pmatrix} 8 & 5 \\ 3 & 2 \end{pmatrix}$

(b) **B**, where $B = \begin{pmatrix} 5 & 3 \\ 6 & 4 \end{pmatrix}$.

(a) $A^{-1} = \begin{pmatrix} 2 & ^-5 \\ ^-3 & 8 \end{pmatrix}$ Determinant is $16 - 15 = 1$

(b) $B^{-1} = \begin{pmatrix} 2 & ^-1 \cdot 5 \\ ^-3 & 2 \cdot 5 \end{pmatrix}$ Determinant is $20 - 18 = 2$

Check your answers by multiplying.

(a) $\begin{pmatrix} 8 & 5 \\ 3 & 2 \end{pmatrix}\begin{pmatrix} 2 & ^-5 \\ ^-3 & 8 \end{pmatrix} = \begin{pmatrix} 1 & 0 \\ 0 & 1 \end{pmatrix}$

(b) $\begin{pmatrix} 5 & 3 \\ 6 & 4 \end{pmatrix}\begin{pmatrix} 2 & ^-1 \cdot 5 \\ ^-3 & 2 \cdot 5 \end{pmatrix} = \begin{pmatrix} 1 & 0 \\ 0 & 1 \end{pmatrix}$

It does not matter whether you multiply the matrix by its inverse or vice versa.

Here is an exam question   ...and its solution

Given the matrices $A = \begin{pmatrix} 6 & 4 \\ 2 & 1 \end{pmatrix}$ and $B = \begin{pmatrix} 3 \\ 5 \end{pmatrix}$, work out

(a) **AB**

(b) A^{-1}, the inverse of **A**.

(a) $\begin{pmatrix} 6 & 4 \\ 2 & 1 \end{pmatrix}\begin{pmatrix} 3 \\ 5 \end{pmatrix} = \begin{pmatrix} 38 \\ 11 \end{pmatrix}$

(b) $\begin{pmatrix} ^-0 \cdot 5 & 2 \\ 1 & ^-3 \end{pmatrix}$ Determinant is $6 - 8 = ^-2$

Now try these exam questions:

1 Given the matrices $A = \begin{pmatrix} 3 & 4 \\ 2 & 4 \end{pmatrix}$ and $B = \begin{pmatrix} 5 \\ 1 \end{pmatrix}$, work out

(a) **AB**

(b) A^{-1}, the inverse of **A**.

2 $A = \begin{pmatrix} 3 & ^-2 \\ 1 & 2 \end{pmatrix}$.

(a) Find the 2×2 matrix **M**, such that $A + M = \begin{pmatrix} 0 & 0 \\ 0 & 0 \end{pmatrix}$.

(b) Find the 2×2 matrix **N**, such that $AN = \begin{pmatrix} 1 & 0 \\ 0 & 1 \end{pmatrix}$.

3 $P = \begin{pmatrix} 1 & 0 \\ x & 0 \end{pmatrix}$, $Q = \begin{pmatrix} 3 & ^-2 \\ ^-2 & 3 \end{pmatrix}$ and $R = \begin{pmatrix} 4 & ^-2 \\ ^-6 & 3 \end{pmatrix}$.

(a) $P + Q = R$. Find the value of x.

(b) Explain why **R** cannot have an inverse matrix.

(c) Find Q^{-1}, the inverse of **Q**.

4 $X = \begin{pmatrix} 3 & 2 \\ ^-4 & ^-1 \end{pmatrix}$, $Y = \begin{pmatrix} 5 & p \\ 2 & ^-4 \end{pmatrix}$ and $Z = \begin{pmatrix} 19 & q \\ ^-22 & 16 \end{pmatrix}$.

(a) If $XY = Z$, find the value of p and the value of q.

(b) Find X^{-1}, the inverse of **X**.

5 $A = \begin{pmatrix} 1 \\ 3 \end{pmatrix}$ and $B = \begin{pmatrix} 3 & ^-4 \\ ^-2 & 5 \end{pmatrix}$.

(a) Explain why it is not possible to work out **AB**.

(b) Work out
(i) B^2
(ii) B^{-1}, the inverse of **B**.

Properties of triangles and other shapes

Exterior angles of triangles

- If one side of a triangle is extended, the angle formed outside the triangle is called an exterior angle.

- The exterior angle of any triangle is equal to the sum of the opposite interior angles. In the diagram d is the exterior angle.

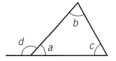

- Proof:
  $a + b + c = 180°$ (angles in a triangle = 180°)
  $a + d = 180°$ (angles on a straight line = 180°)
  Therefore $d = b + c$.

> You need to use the angle facts you already know about triangles, straight lines and parallel lines

Example

Calculate the size of the angles marked with letters. Give reasons for the answers.

(a)

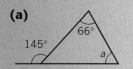

(b)

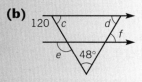

(a) $a = 79°$ (exterior angle = sum of opposite interior angles)

(b) $c = 60°$ (angles on a straight line = 180°)
    $d = 72°$ (angles in a triangle = 180°)
    $e = 120°$ (corresponding angles are equal)
    $f = 72°$ (alternate angles are equal)

Now try these:

Calculate the size of the angles marked with letters in questions 1 to 3. Give reasons for your answers.

1

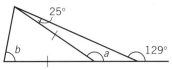

2

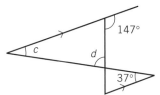

3

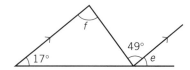

4 Find angle g in terms of x. Show all the steps of your working.

Polygons

- The sum of the exterior angles of any polygon is 360°.
- If the interior angles are required it is easiest to work with the exterior angles. Then use the fact that, at any vertex, the sum of the interior and the exterior angles is 180°.

> It is useful to know that the sum of the interior angles of:
> a quadrilateral is 360°
> a pentagon is 540°
> a hexagon is 720°.

Example

A regular polygon has 12 sides. Work out:
(a) the size of each interior angle
(b) the sum of the interior angles.

Each exterior angle $= \dfrac{360}{12} = 30°$

(a) Each interior angle $= 180 - 30 = 150°$.
(b) The sum of the interior angles
    $= 150 \times 12 = 1800°$.

Now try these:

5 Find the interior angle of a regular octagon.

6 Three interior angles of a quadrilateral are 112°, 65° and 79°. Find the size of the fourth angle.

7 A regular polygon has an interior angle of 156°. How many sides has the polygon?

8 A pentagon has four interior angles of 75°, 96°, 125° and 142°. Find the size of the fifth interior angle.

> A non-regular polygon with 12 sides will have the same interior angle sum as a regular 12-sided polygon. This needs to be used when finding one of the angles when the rest are given.

Congruent and similar triangles

For triangles to be congruent:

- corresponding angles are equal.
- corresponding sides are equal.

For triangles to be similar:

- corresponding angles are equal
- corresponding sides have lengths in proportion.

Now try these:

9 Prove that these triangles are similar.

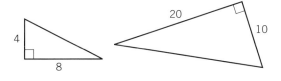

10 Triangles LMN and PQR are similar.
Find the lengths of the missing sides.

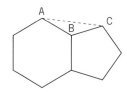

Example

(a) Prove that triangle ABC is similar to triangle PQR.

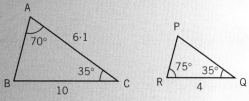

(b) Find the length of PQ.

(a) Angle ABC − 180 − 70 − 35 = 75
Angle RPQ = 180 − 70 − 35 = 70
Triangles are similar as corresponding angles are equal.

(b) $\frac{PQ}{4} = \frac{6.1}{10}$

PQ = 2·4 (1 d.p.)

Here is an exam question   ...and its solution

The sketch shows a regular pentagon and a regular hexagon with equal length sides.

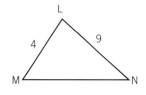

(a) Work out the size of one interior angle of:
 (i) the pentagon
 (ii) the hexagon.

(b) Work out the sizes of the angles in triangle ABC.

(a) (i) 108°

(ii) 120°

(b) 24°, 24°, 132°

exterior angle = $\frac{360}{5}$
 = 72°
interior angle = 180 − 72
 = 108°
exterior angle = $\frac{360}{6}$
 = 60°
interior angle = 180 − 60
 = 120°

In triangle ABC, angle ABC
 = 360 − 120 − 108
 = 132°
It is isosceles as AB = BC.
So angles BAC and BCA
 = $\frac{180 - 132}{2}$
 = $\frac{48}{2}$
 = 24°

Now try these exam questions:

1 Here is a sketch of a regular
pentagon, centre O.

  (a) Work out *x*.
  (b) What type of triangle is OAB?

2 In the diagram BC is parallel to DE.

  Find the size of *x* and *y*.
  Give reasons for your answers.

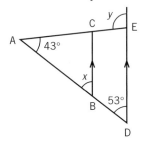

3 The interior angle of an *n*-sided regular polygon is 48°
more than the interior angle of a regular hexagon.
Find the value of *n*.

4

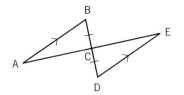

Work out the size of angles *x* and *y*.

5

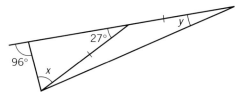

Find the size of angles *x* and *y*, and give reasons for
your answers.

6

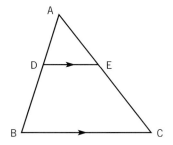

In the diagram AB is parallel to DE and BC = CD.
State, with reasons, which triangle is congruent to
triangle ABC.

7 (a) In triangle ABC, DE is parallel to BC.
     Prove that triangles ADE and ABC are similar.
  (b) D divides AB in the ratio 1 : 3.
     DE is 3 cm.
     Calculate the length of BC.

Pythagoras and trigonometry

Pythagoras' theorem

- You should be familiar with Pythagoras' theorem:

$$a^2 = b^2 + c^2$$

- Remember to:
  1. Label the triangle, using letters for the sides.
  2. Write down the rule.
  3. Substitute the actual values for the sides.
  4. Do any rearrangement, if necessary.

- You also need to remember the ratios: sin, cos and tan.

$$\tan x = \frac{O}{A}$$

$$\sin x = \frac{O}{H}$$

$$\cos x = \frac{A}{H}$$

Example

Calculate the length of the hypotenuse in this triangle:

$$a^2 = b^2 + c^2$$
$$a^2 = 8^2 + 6^2$$
$$a^2 = 100$$
$$a = \sqrt{100}$$
$$= 10\,\text{cm}$$

Example

Calculate the length of the unknown side in this triangle.

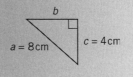

$$a^2 = b^2 + c^2$$
$$8^2 = b^2 + 4^2$$
$$b^2 = 64 - 16$$
$$= 48$$
$$b = \sqrt{48}$$
$$= 6{\cdot}9\,\text{cm, to 1 d.p.}$$

Now try these:

1 Find:
  (a) AB
  (b) the angle ACB.

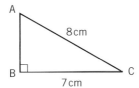

2 Find:
  (a) DE
  (b) EF.

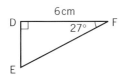

3 Find:
  (a) MN
  (b) the angle LMN.

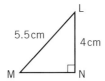

4 A ladder of length L is placed against a vertical wall. The ground is horizontal, the foot of the ladder is 3 m from the wall and the top is 8 m vertically above the ground.

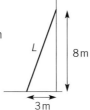

  (a) Find the length of the ladder.
  (b) The foot of the ladder is moved a further 2 m from the base of the wall. Find the distance the ladder moves down the wall.

5 Find the angle PQR.

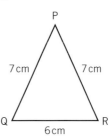

6 ABCD is the side of the frame of the goal used by a football club.

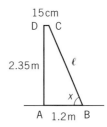

  (a) Calculate the length of the sloping strut, ℓ, joining C to B.
  (b) Calculate the angle, x, that CB makes with the ground.

Sine and cosine rules

- You should know the sine and cosine rules.

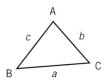

In this triangle the sine rule is $\dfrac{a}{\sin A} = \dfrac{b}{\sin B} = \dfrac{c}{\sin C}$.
The cosine rule is
$a^2 = b^2 + c^2 - 2bc\cos A$,
$b^2 = c^2 + a^2 - 2ac\cos B$,
$c^2 = a^2 + b^2 - 2ab\cos C$.

- The area of the triangle is given by $\dfrac{1}{2}ab\sin C$
  or by $\sqrt{s(s-a)(s-b)(s-c)}$, where
  $s = \dfrac{1}{2}(a+b+c)$.

Example

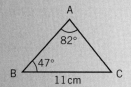

(a) Find the lengths of AC and AB and the size of angle ACB.
(b) Calculate the area of triangle ABC.

(a) $\dfrac{a}{\sin A} = \dfrac{b}{\sin B}$

$\dfrac{11}{\sin 82°} = \dfrac{b}{\sin 47°}$

$b = \dfrac{11 \times \sin 47°}{\sin 82°} = 8.12\,\text{cm}$

AC = 8.12 cm
Angle ACB = 180° − 47° − 82° = 51°

$\dfrac{c}{\sin C} = \dfrac{a}{\sin A}$

$c = \dfrac{11 \times \sin 51°}{\sin 82°} = 8.63\,\text{cm}$

AB = 8.63 cm

(b) Using $\dfrac{1}{2}ab\sin C$,

Area = $\dfrac{1}{2} \times 11 \times 8.63 \times \sin 47° = 34.7\,\text{cm}^2$

Using $\sqrt{s(s-a)(s-b)(s-c)}$,

Area = $\sqrt{13.875 \times 2.875 \times 5.755 \times 5.245}$
     = 34.7 cm²

Now try these:

7 Find:
  (a) AB
  (b) the angle ABC.

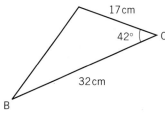

8 In triangle XYZ angle YXZ = 130°, angle XZY = 28° and YZ = 14 cm.

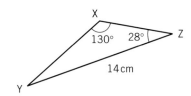

Calculate the length of XZ.

9 A submarine is on a bearing of 275° from a ship, S, and on a bearing of 312° from a second ship, P. Ship P is 200 m due south of ship S.

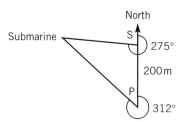

Calculate the distance from the submarine to the second ship, P.

Here is an exam question   ...and its solution

A ship sails from a port P a distance of 7 km on a bearing of 310° and then a further 11 km on a bearing of 070° to arrive at a point X where it anchors.

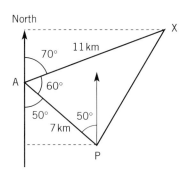

(a) Calculate the distance from P to X.

(b) Calculate how far east of P the point X is.

(a) 9.64 km

$$PX^2 = 7^2 + 11^2 - 2 \times 7 \times 11\cos60$$
$$= 49 + 121 - 77$$
$$PX = 9{\cdot}64$$

(b) 4·97 km

Distance East = $11\sin70 - 7\sin50$
$$= 4{\cdot}97$$

Now try these exam questions:

1 To assist hang gliders a large orange arrow is placed on the ground to show the wind direction.

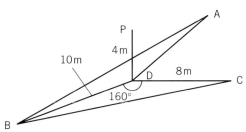

The triangles ABD and CBD are congruent.
BD = 10 m, DC = 8 m, angle BDC = 160°
(a) Calculate the length of BC.
A vertical pole, DP, of height 4 m, with a flag at the top, is fixed at D and held by wires from A, B and C.
(b) Calculate the length of wire from A to P.

2 In triangle ACB, AC = 3 m, BC = 8 m and angle ACB = 15°.

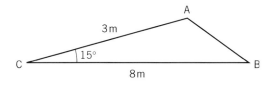

(a) Calculate the length of AB.
(b) Calculate the area of triangle ABC.

3

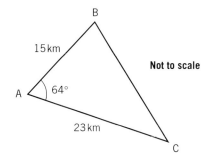

The diagram shows the position of three ships A, B and C.
(a) Calculate the distance BC.
(b) An air–sea rescue search has to be made of the region inside triangle ABC. Calculate the area to be searched.

Properties of circles

Sectors and segments

- The shaded parts are called 'minor' sector and 'minor' segment.
- The unshaded parts are called 'major' sector and 'major' segment.

 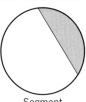

Sector   Segment

Tangent properties of circles

- The tangent at any point on a circle is at right angles to the radius at that point.
- The two tangents from a point outside a circle to the circle are equal in length.

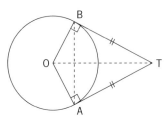

Figure A

So angle TAO = angle TBO = 90°, and TA = TB.

Example

(a) In Figure A, TA = 9 cm and TO = 10 cm. Find the radius of the circle.
(b) Angle ATB = 50°. Find angle TAB.

(a) Since angle TAO = 90°, use Pythagoras.
$OA^2 + 9^2 = 10^2$
$OA = \sqrt{(100 - 81)}$ cm = 4·36 cm
(b) Since TA = TB, triangle TAB is isosceles.
Angle TAB = $\frac{1}{2}(180° - 50°) = 65°$

Chord properties of circles

The perpendicular from the centre of a circle to a chord bisects the chord.

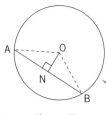

Figure B

So AN = BN.

Example

Angle AOB = 120° and the radius of the circle = 5 cm. Find AB.

Angle BON = $\frac{1}{2}(120°) = 60°$,
$\frac{BN}{OB} = \sin 60°$, so BN = $5 \times \sin 60° = 4·33$ cm.

Since AN = BN, AB = $4·33 \times 2 = 8·66$ cm.

The reason is that OA and OB are both radii, so triangle OAB is isosceles. Since ON is perpendicular to AB it is the line of symmetry for the triangle. Therefore AN = BN.

Now try these:

Questions 1 to 3 refer to Figure A.

1 TA = 15 cm and AO = 8 cm. Calculate the length of TO.

2 TA = 7 cm and angle ATB = 70°. Calculate the radius of the circle.

3 Angle OAB = 25°. Find angle ATB.

4 In Figure B, ON = 4 cm and OB = 6 cm. Calculate the length AB.

5 PQ and PR are tangents which touch a circle, centre O, at Q and R respectively. If angle PQR = 70°, find angle QRO.

Draw a diagram.

Angle properties of circles

- The angle subtended by an arc at the centre is twice the angle subtended at the circumference.

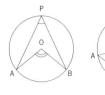

Figure C　　　　**Figure D**

Angle AOB = 2 × angle APB.
Reflex angle AOB = 2 × angle AQB.

- The angle in a semi-circle is a right angle.

Angle ACB = 90°

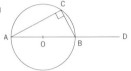

Figure E

- Angles in the same segment are equal.

Angle ADB = angle ACB and angle DAC = angle DBC.

Figure F

- Opposite angles of a cyclic quadrilateral add up to 180°.

Angle ABC + angle CDA = 180°
and
angle BAD + angle BCD = 180°.

Figure G

Example

In Figure C angle AOB = 68°.
Find angle APB.

Angle APB = $\frac{1}{2}$ angle AOB = $\frac{1}{2}$ × 68° = 34°.

Example

In Figure D angle AQB = 115°.

Find　(a) reflex angle AOB
　　　(b) angle AOB.

(a) Reflex angle AOB = 2 × angle AQB
　　　　　　　　= 2 × 115° = 230°
(b) Angle AOB = 360° − 230° = 130°

Example

In Figure E angle CAO = 38° and O is the centre of the circle. AOBD is a straight line.
Find angle CBD.

Angle ACB = 90°.
So angle CBA = 180° − 38° − 90° = 52°
So angle CBD = 180° − 52° = 128°

Example

In Figure F, angle ACB = 35°. Find angle ADB. Give your reasons.

Angle ADB = 35° because angles ACB and ADB are angles in the same segment.

Example

In Figure G, angle BCD = 102°. Find angle BAD. Give your reasons.

Angle BAD = 180° − 102° = 78° because angles BCD and BAD are opposite angles of a cyclic quadrilateral.

When giving reasons, use the standard phrases, e.g.
'angles in a semi-circle',
'angles in the same segment',
'angle at centre = twice angle at circumference',
'opposite angles of a cyclic quadrilateral'.

Now try these:

6 Find:
(a) angle CAD
(b) angle CBD.

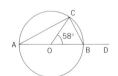

7 Find angle CDE.
Give your reasons.

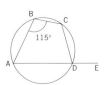

8 In Figure F, explain why triangle DXA is similar to triangle CXB. Give reasons for each of your statements.

9 Find angles *a*, *b* and *c*.

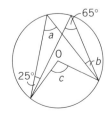

Here is an exam question   ...and its solution

O is the centre of the circle and angle ATB is 50°.
TA and TB are tangents.

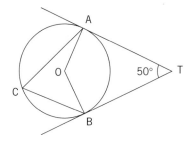

(a) Find angle AOB.
(b) Find angle ACB, giving a reason for your answer.

(a) 130°	Angle OAT = angle OBT = 90° Angle AOB = 360 − 90 − 90 − 50 = 130°.
(b) 65°	Angle ACB = ½ × 130 = 65°. Because angle at centre = twice angle at circumference.

Now try these exam questions:

1

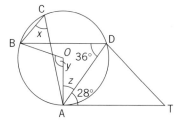

A, B, C and D are points on a circle, centre O.
TA is a tangent to the circle. Find the size of each
of the angles labelled x, y and z in the diagram.
Write down the circle property you used to obtain
your answer.

2

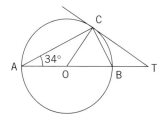

The diagram shows a circle, centre O. The diameter AB
is produced to T and TC is a tangent to the circle.
Calculate: **(a)** angle OCB **(b)** angle CBT **(c)** angle CTA.

3 In the diagram, O is the
centre of the circle, PT is
the tangent to the circle at P
and Q is the point
where the line OT cuts the
circle. Calculate the
sizes of the angles marked a,
b, c, and d.

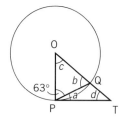

4 In the diagram, O is the
centre of the circle, AD
is a diameter and AB is
a tangent.
Angle ACE = x°. Find,
in terms of x, the size of:
(a) angle ADE
(b) angle DAE
(c) angle EAB
(d) angle AOE.

5 (a)

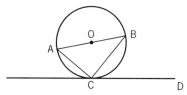

AB is a diameter of the circle centre O. CD is
a tangent touching the circle at C.
Write down the size of angle ACB giving your
reason.

(b)

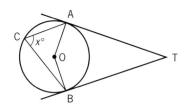

TA and TB are tangents to the circle centre O.
Angle ACB = x°. Find the size of angle ATB in
terms of x.

3D shapes

Prisms

- A prism is a 3D shape with a constant cross-section.
- Examples of prisms are:

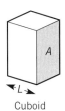 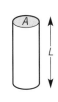

| Cuboid | Cylinder | Triangular prism |

- For all prisms:
  Volume = area of cross-section × length
  $V = A \times L$
- The surface area of a prism is the total area of all the surfaces of the prism.

> Don't forget to include the units with your answer.

Now try these:

1 The volume of water in the tank is 2000 cm³. Find the depth of the water.

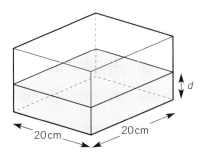

2 Find the volume of this bar of gold.

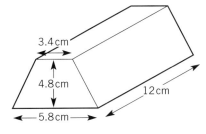

Example
Find the volume and surface area of this prism.

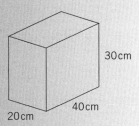

Volume = area of cross-section × length
  = (40 × 30) × 20
  = 240 000 cm³
Surface area = 2 × top + 2 × side + 2 × front
  = 2(20 × 40) + 2(30 × 40) + 2(20 × 30)
  = 5200 cm²

Example
The volume of this packet of sweets is 68 cm³. Find its length.

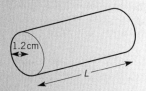

Volume = area of cross-section × length
  68 = (π × 1·2²) × L
  $L = \dfrac{68}{(\pi \times 1{\cdot}2^2)} = 15$ cm

3 The volume of this cylinder is 50 cm³. Find the radius of the circular end.

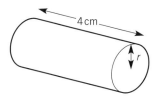

Pyramids, cones and spheres

- A pyramid is any 3D shape which goes up to a point. The shape of the base is usually part of the name of the pyramid.
  $V = \frac{1}{3} \times$ area of base × height

Example
A pyramid has a square base of side 4 m and is 9 m high. Calculate the volume of the pyramid.

$V = \frac{1}{3} \times (4 \times 4) \times 9$
  = 48 m³

- A pyramid shape with a circular base is a cone.
  $V = \frac{1}{3}\pi r^2 h$
  Curved surface area = $\pi r \ell$

Example

Find the height of a cone with volume
2·5 litres and base radius 10 cm.

$$2500 = \frac{1}{3} \times \pi \times 10^2 \times h$$
$$h = \frac{3 \times 2500}{\pi \times 100}$$
$$h = 23·9 \text{ cm}$$

- A sphere has volume
  $V = \frac{4}{3}\pi r^3$
  Surface area = $4\pi r^2$

Example

A sphere has a surface area of 500 cm².
Calculate the radius of the sphere.

$$500 = 4\pi r^2$$
$$r^2 = \frac{500}{4\pi}$$
$$r = 6·3 \text{ cm}$$

Now try these:

4 Find the volume of a hemisphere of radius 6 cm.

5 Find the slant height of a cone which has a base radius
  of 4 cm and a **total** surface area of 200 cm².

6 A piece of cheese is in the shape of a cuboid.

  One corner is cut off. The cut goes through one corner, A, and the midpoints, B
  and C of two sides, as shown.
  Calculate the volume of the remaining piece of cheese.

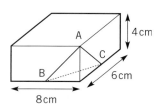

Volume and surface area of similar shapes

For similar shapes:
Area scale factor = (length scale factor)²
Volume scale factor = (length scale factor)³.

Example

Two similar cylinders have heights 8 cm
and 16 cm.
(a) The smaller has a volume of 60 cm³.
     Find the volume of the larger.
(b) Another similar cylinder has a volume of
     202·5 cm³. Find its height.

(a) Length scale factor = $\frac{16}{8}$ = 2.
     Volume = $60 \times 2^3 = 480 \text{ cm}^3$.
(b) Length scale factor = $\left(\frac{202·5}{60}\right)^{\frac{1}{3}}$ = 1.5
     Height = $8 \times 1.5 = 12 \text{ cm}$.

Now try these:

7 A toy van is made to a scale 1 : 50.
  (a) The actual van is 2·4 m wide. How wide is the model?
  (b) The front window of the model has an area of 4 cm². What is the window area of the actual van?

8 Two similar objects have volumes 24 cm³ and 81 cm³. The surface area of the larger object is 540 cm². Find the
  surface area of the smaller object.

Here is an exam question ...and its solution

Find the volume of this greenhouse.
The ends are semi-circles.

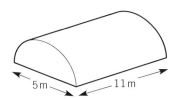

108 m^3

Volume = area of cross-section × length
$$= \left(\frac{1}{2} \times \pi \times 2{\cdot}5^2\right) \times 11$$
$$= 108$$

Now try these exam questions:

1 Find the volume of this trunk. The end face of the lid is a semi-circle

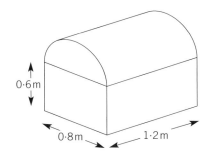

2 The volume of this triangular prism is 42 cm^3. Find its surface area.

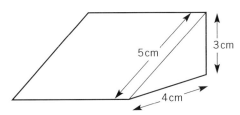

3 An ice cream cone has height 11 cm and radius 3·5 cm. Ice cream completely fills the cone and forms a hemisphere on the top of the cone. Neglecting the thickness of the cone, calculate the volume of ice cream.

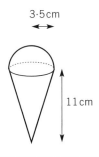

4 The four slant edges of this square base pyramid are 6 cm long. The four edges of the base are each 4 cm long. Calculate the volume of the pyramid.

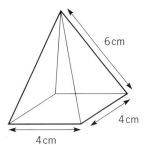

5 Three similar suitcases each have dimensions which are 25% greater than those of the next smaller suitcase.
   (a) The middle suitcase is 40 cm tall. How tall is the smallest suitcase?
   (b) The middle suitcase has a volume of $32\,000 \text{ cm}^3$. Calculate the volume of the largest suitcase.

6 A cone has height 10 cm and base radius 4 cm. A smaller cone with height 5 cm is cut from the top of the cone. The part that is left is called a *frustum*.
   (a) What is the radius of the base of the smaller cone?
   (b) Calculate the volume of the frustum.

Transformations and coordinates

Transformations

- You need to know about six types of transformation: reflection, rotation, translation, enlargement, stretch and shear.
- You may be asked to follow instructions to draw the result of a transformation or combination of transformations.
- You may be asked to describe a transformation which has taken place. When describing, give the type of transformation first, then the extra information required.

Reflection

- For a reflection the image is the same shape and size as the object, but is reversed.
- Each point on the image is the same distance from the mirror line as the corresponding point on the object.
- When describing a reflection, state the mirror line.

Rotation

- For a rotation the image is the same shape and size as the object, but is turned round.
- Each point on the image is the same distance from the centre of rotation as the corresponding point on the object.
- To find a centre of rotation, tracing paper may often be used. If construction is required, draw the perpendicular bisectors of lines joining corresponding points. Where they meet is the centre of rotation.
- When describing a rotation, state the centre of rotation, the angle and the direction – clockwise or anticlockwise.

Translation

- For a translation the image is the same shape and size as the object and is the same way up.
- Each point on the image has moved the same distance and direction from its corresponding point on the object.
- When describing a translation, state the column vector, or how many units the object has moved in each direction. For instance, translate by the column vector $\binom{-2}{5}$ means move two units across to the left and five units up.

Example

Here, the object has been translated by $\binom{-2}{5}$.

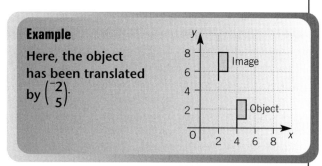

Enlargement

- For an enlargement the image is the same shape as the object but each length on the image is the corresponding length on the object multiplied by the scale factor.
- The distance of each point on the object from the centre of enlargement is multiplied by the scale factor to find the distance from the centre of the corresponding point on the image.
- To find the centre of enlargement, join corresponding points on the object and image and extend the lines until they meet.
- When describing an enlargement, state the centre of enlargement and the scale factor.
- If the scale factor is negative, each point is transformed to a point on the other side of the centre.

Example

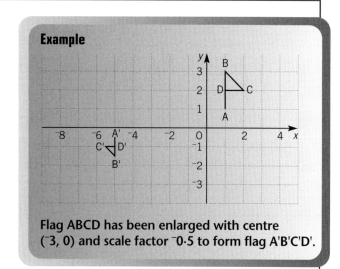

Flag ABCD has been enlarged with centre (⁻3, 0) and scale factor ⁻0·5 to form flag A'B'C'D'.

Now try these:

1 Draw axes from 0 to 5 for *x* and *y*. Plot the points (3, 1) (3, 2) (3, 3) and (4, 2) and join them to form flag A. Enlarge flag A with centre (1, 0) and scale factor $\frac{1}{2}$. Label the image B.

2 Look at the graph on the right. Describe the transformation which maps:

(a) E onto A
(b) A onto D
(c) A onto B
(d) B onto A
(e) F onto G
(f) B onto H
(g) D onto E
(h) C onto F
(i) E onto D
(j) C onto E
(k) A onto H.

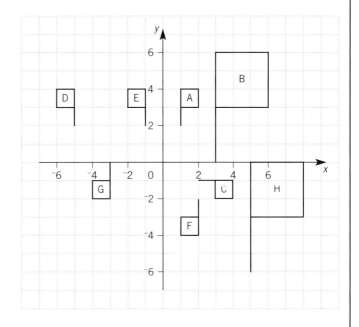

Stretch

- When an object is stretched usually it is lengthened in one direction only – either parallel to the *x*-axis or parallel to the *y*-axis. (However an object may be stretched in both directions.)

- A stretch is defined by three pieces of information: the scale factor, the fixed line (sometimes called the **invariant** line) and the direction of the stretch.

- Every point on the invariant line remains fixed.

Example

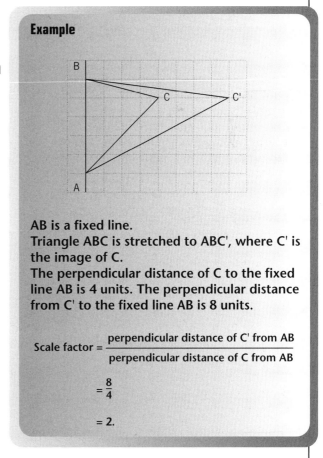

AB is a fixed line.
Triangle ABC is stretched to ABC', where C' is the image of C.
The perpendicular distance of C to the fixed line AB is 4 units. The perpendicular distance from C' to the fixed line AB is 8 units.

$$\text{Scale factor} = \frac{\text{perpendicular distance of C' from AB}}{\text{perpendicular distance of C from AB}}$$

$$= \frac{8}{4}$$

$$= 2.$$

Now try these:

3 In these diagrams AB is the fixed line.
Calculate the scale factor for each of the following stretches:

(a)

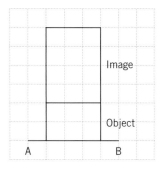

(b)

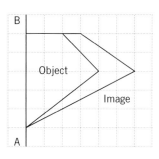

4 For each of these drawings, give the equation of the fixed line and calculate the stretch factor.

(a)

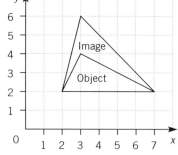

(b)

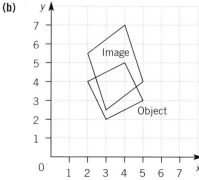

Shear

- A shear is the name given to a transformation when it appears that an object is made from different layers and each layer slides a different amount relative to a fixed line.

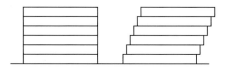

- A shear is defined by three pieces of information: the shear factor, the fixed line and the direction of the shear.

Example

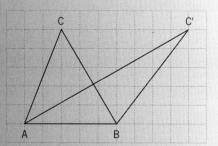

AB is the fixed line; the position of every point on the line is the same before and after the shear.
The perpendicular distance of C from the fixed line is 5 units. The effect of this shear is to move C to C′, 7 units to the right.

$$\text{Shear factor} = \frac{\text{distance a point moves due to the shear}}{\text{perpendicular distance of the point from the fixed line}}$$

$$= \frac{7}{5}$$

$$= 1\cdot4.$$

Now try these:

5 In these diagrams AB is the fixed line. Calculate the shear factor for each of the following shears.

(a)

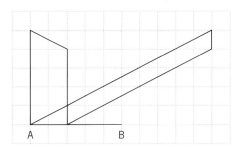

(b)

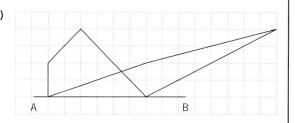

Combining transformations

- Two or more transformations may follow each other.

Take care that you label diagrams carefully and transform the shape you have been asked to and not another one!

- You may be asked to describe a single transformation which would have the same effect as two transformations that you have done.

Now try these:

In questions 6–9, carry out the transformations on a simple shape of your choice, then describe the single transformation that is equivalent to the combination.

6 A translation of $\begin{pmatrix} 1 \\ 4 \end{pmatrix}$ followed by a translation of $\begin{pmatrix} 2 \\ -3 \end{pmatrix}$.

7 A reflection in the line $x = 3$ followed by a reflection in the line $y = 2$.

8 A reflection in the x-axis followed by a rotation through 90° anticlockwise about (0, 0).

9 A rotation through 90° anticlockwise about (0, 0) followed by a reflection in the x-axis.

10 (a) A triangle ABC maps onto triangle ABC' after a shear of factor 2 to the right where line AB is the fixed line.
(b) Triangle ABC' is then reflected in the x-axis onto triangle A"B"C".
(c) Triangle A"B"C" is mapped onto A"B"C" after a shear of factor 2 to the right, with the fixed line $x = {}^-4$.
Copy the diagram and show all the transformations.

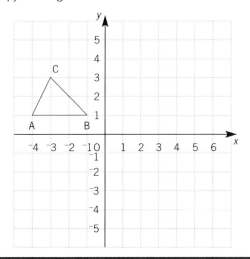

Example

B is the image of A after reflection in the y-axis. C is the image of B after reflection in the x-axis. Describe the single transformation which maps A directly onto C.

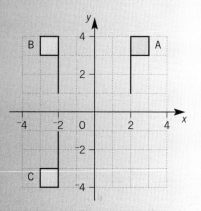

A has been rotated through 180° with centre (0, 0).

11 (a) Shape ABCDE is mapped onto shape A'B'C'D'E' by a stretch of scale factor 2 to the right from the fixed line $x = {}^-7$.
(b) Shape A'B'C'D'E' is then reflected in the line $x = 0$ onto shape A"B"C"D"E".
(c) Shape A"B"C"D"E" is then mapped onto A"'B"'C"'D"'E"' by a shear of factor 1 relative to the fixed line $y = 4$.
Copy the diagram and show all the transformations.

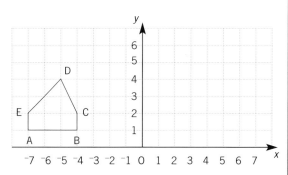

Transformations and matrices

- The coordinates of a shape can be given by a matrix. For example, the quadrilateral A(1, 1), B(3, 1), C(3, 2), D(1, 3) can be defined by the matrix

$$\begin{matrix} \text{A} & \text{B} & \text{C} & \text{D} \end{matrix}$$
$$\begin{pmatrix} 1 & 3 & 3 & 1 \\ 1 & 1 & 2 & 3 \end{pmatrix}$$

- A transformation can also be given by a matrix, for example

$$\begin{pmatrix} ^-1 & 0 \\ 0 & 1 \end{pmatrix}$$

- Multiplying the two matrices gives the coordinates of the image.

$$\begin{pmatrix} ^-1 & 0 \\ 0 & 1 \end{pmatrix}\begin{pmatrix} 1 & 3 & 3 & 1 \\ 1 & 1 & 2 & 3 \end{pmatrix} = \begin{pmatrix} ^-1 & ^-3 & ^-3 & ^-1 \\ 1 & 1 & 2 & 3 \end{pmatrix}$$

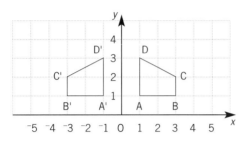

- The following table gives the matrices for some common transformations.

Matrix	Transformation
$\begin{pmatrix} 1 & 0 \\ 0 & ^-1 \end{pmatrix}$	Reflection in the x-axis
$\begin{pmatrix} 0 & 1 \\ 1 & 0 \end{pmatrix}$	Reflection in the line $y = x$
$\begin{pmatrix} ^-1 & 0 \\ 0 & ^-1 \end{pmatrix}$	Rotation of 180° about the origin
$\begin{pmatrix} 1 & p \\ 0 & 1 \end{pmatrix}$	Shear, parallel to the x-axis, with fixed line the x-axis, and shear factor p
$\begin{pmatrix} p & 0 \\ 0 & 1 \end{pmatrix}$	Stretch of scale factor p, parallel to the x-axis with the y-axis as the fixed line
$\begin{pmatrix} p & 0 \\ 0 & p \end{pmatrix}$	Enlargement of scale factor p and centre (0, 0)

$\begin{pmatrix} ^-1 & 0 \\ 0 & 1 \end{pmatrix}$	Reflection in the y-axis
$\begin{pmatrix} 0 & ^-1 \\ ^-1 & 0 \end{pmatrix}$	Reflection in the line $y = ^-x$
$\begin{pmatrix} 0 & ^-1 \\ ^-1 & 0 \end{pmatrix}$	Rotation of 90° anticlockwise about the origin
$\begin{pmatrix} 1 & 0 \\ p & 1 \end{pmatrix}$	Shear, parallel to the y-axis, with fixed line the y-axis, and shear factor p
$\begin{pmatrix} p & 0 \\ 0 & q \end{pmatrix}$	Stretch of scale factor p, parallel to the x-axis with the y-axis as the fixed line and stretch of scale factor q parallel to the y-axis with the x-axis as the fixed line

Example

Triangle ABC is reflected in the y-axis to map onto triangle A'B'C'.
Triangle A'B'C' is rotated through 180° about (0, 0) to map onto A"B"C".
Use matrices to find the single transformation equivalent to these two transformations.

Reflection in the y-axis is produced by the matrix $\begin{pmatrix} ^-1 & 0 \\ 0 & 1 \end{pmatrix}$.

Rotation of 180° is produced by the matrix $\begin{pmatrix} ^-1 & 0 \\ 0 & ^-1 \end{pmatrix}$.

The single transformation equivalent to these two transformations is obtained by multiplying the matrices.

$$\begin{pmatrix} ^-1 & 0 \\ 0 & ^-1 \end{pmatrix}\begin{pmatrix} ^-1 & 0 \\ 0 & 1 \end{pmatrix} = \begin{pmatrix} 1 & 0 \\ 0 & ^-1 \end{pmatrix}$$

This is the matrix for a reflection in the x-axis.

Example

Triangle PQR with coordinates P(1, 1), Q(4, 2) and R(2, 4) is mapped onto P'Q'R' using the matrix A, $\begin{pmatrix} 2 & 1 \\ 1 & 2 \end{pmatrix}$.

Triangle P'Q'R' is then transformed onto P"Q"R" using matrix B, $\begin{pmatrix} ^-1 & 0 \\ 0 & 1 \end{pmatrix}$.

(a) What single matrix would map triangle PQR onto triangle P"Q"R"?
(b) What are the coordinates of triangle P"Q"R"?

(a) The single transformation has the matrix BA = $\begin{pmatrix} ^-1 & 0 \\ 0 & 1 \end{pmatrix}\begin{pmatrix} 2 & 1 \\ 1 & 2 \end{pmatrix} = \begin{pmatrix} ^-2 & ^-1 \\ 1 & 2 \end{pmatrix}$.

(b) $\begin{pmatrix} ^-2 & ^-1 \\ 1 & 2 \end{pmatrix}\begin{pmatrix} 1 & 4 & 2 \\ 1 & 2 & 4 \end{pmatrix} = \begin{pmatrix} ^-3 & ^-10 & ^-8 \\ 1 & 2 & 10 \end{pmatrix}$

The coordinates are P"(–3, 3), Q"(–10, 8) and R"(–8, 10).

Check:

$$\begin{pmatrix} 2 & 1 \\ 1 & 2 \end{pmatrix}\begin{pmatrix} 1 & 4 & 2 \\ 1 & 2 & 4 \end{pmatrix} = \begin{pmatrix} 3 & 10 & 8 \\ 3 & 8 & 10 \end{pmatrix}$$

$$\begin{pmatrix} ^-1 & 0 \\ 0 & 1 \end{pmatrix}\begin{pmatrix} 3 & 10 & 8 \\ 3 & 8 & 10 \end{pmatrix} = \begin{pmatrix} ^-3 & ^-10 & ^-8 \\ 3 & 8 & 10 \end{pmatrix}$$

- Notice that there is a form of 'symmetry' to the matrices dealing with a particular type of transformation.

> If you are unsure what effect multiplying by a matrix will have then sketch the unit square and multiply its matrix $\begin{pmatrix} 0 & 0 & 1 & 1 \\ 0 & 1 & 1 & 0 \end{pmatrix}$ by the matrix you wish to check.

- When an object is transformed by a series of transformation matrices these matrices can be replaced by a single matrix which maps the original object onto the final image.

  Thus if $A = \begin{pmatrix} 2 & 1 \\ 1 & 2 \end{pmatrix}$ and $B = \begin{pmatrix} ^-1 & 0 \\ 0 & 1 \end{pmatrix}$ the final transformation can be found using the matrix determined by multiplying A and B together *in the correct order*, that is A followed by B.

  This is written as BA.

  $$BA = \begin{pmatrix} ^-1 & 0 \\ 0 & 1 \end{pmatrix}\begin{pmatrix} ^-2 & 1 \\ 1 & 2 \end{pmatrix} = \begin{pmatrix} ^-2 & ^-1 \\ 1 & 2 \end{pmatrix}$$

  Remember, in matrix multiplication the order matters.

Now try these:

12 A square ABCD has vertices at A(2, 0), B(4, 0), C(4, 2) and D(2, 2).

The matrix $P = \begin{pmatrix} 1 & 0 \\ 0 & ^-1 \end{pmatrix}$ and the matrix $Q = \begin{pmatrix} 0 & 1 \\ ^-1 & 0 \end{pmatrix}$.

(a) Give the coordinates of A'B'C'D' when ABCD is transformed using matrix P.

(b) Give the coordinates of A"B"C"D" when ABCD is transformed using matrix Q.

(c) Give the coordinates of A'''B'''C'''D''' when A'B'C'D' is transformed using matrix Q.

(d) Find the matrices R and S where R = QP and S = PQ.

(e) Find the coordinates of the image of ABCD under the transformation given by R.

(f) Find the coordinates of ABCD under the transformation given by S.

13 The vertices of a triangle P are (2, 1), (4, 1) and (4, 4).

The matrix $M = \begin{pmatrix} ^-1 & 0 \\ 0 & ^-1 \end{pmatrix}$ and the matrix $N = \begin{pmatrix} ^-1 & 0 \\ 0 & 1 \end{pmatrix}$.

(a) (i) Find the coordinates of the image of P under the transformation M, i.e. M(P).

(ii) Describe the transformation produced by this matrix.

(b) (i) Find the coordinates of the image of P under the transformation NM, i.e. NM(P).

(ii) Describe the single transformation produced by these matrices.

Calculating with coordinates

- To find the midpoint of the line joining A and B, find the mean of their coordinates.
- To find the length AB use Pythagoras' theorem.

Now try these:

14 Find:
  (i) the midpoint of AB and
  (ii) the length of AB for the following coordinates.
    (a) A is (1, 2) and B is (8, 6)
    (b) A is ($^-$1, 2) and B is (8, $^-$6)
    (c) A is ($^-$3, $^-$4) and B is (5, 2).

Example

When A is (1, 5) and B is (7, 2),

midpoint of AB is $\left(\dfrac{1+7}{2}, \dfrac{5+2}{2}\right) = (4, 3 \cdot 5)$

$AB^2 = 6^2 + 3^2 = 45$

$AB = \sqrt{45} = 6 \cdot 7$ units to 1 d.p.

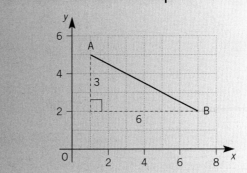

Length, area and volume

- To distinguish between formulae for length, area and volume, consider the dimensions of the formula.
- When a shape is enlarged with scale factor n, its area is enlarged with scale factor n^2.
- When a 3D shape is enlarged with scale factor n, its volume is enlarged with scale factor n^3.

Example

A 2 cm by 3 cm rectangle has area 6 cm². When enlarged by scale factor 4, the rectangle measures 8 cm by 12 cm and has area 96 cm².

The area has been enlarged by a scale factor of 16, or 4².

Now try these:

15 r and h are lengths. State whether each formula could represent an area, a volume or neither.

(a) $\dfrac{\pi h^3}{2r}$ (c) $3r(r+h)^2$

(b) $2r^2(3h+r^2)$

16 A triangle has area 4 cm². The triangle is enlarged with scale factor 1·5. What is the area of the enlarged triangle?

17 A water bottle holds 1 litre. What is the capacity of a similar bottle half as high?

18 A model of a theatre set is built to a scale of 1:20.
(a) A rug on the model has area 40 cm². Find the area of the rug on the actual set.
(b) A cupboard on the set has volume 0·4 m³. Calculate the volume of the cupboard on the model.

Here is an exam question   ...and its solution

Triangle T is rotated 90° clockwise about the point (0, 0). Its image is triangle S. Triangle S is reflected in the y-axis. Its image is triangle R.

(a) Draw triangle S and triangle R on the diagram. Label each triangle clearly.

(b) Describe a **single** transformation that maps R onto T.

(a)
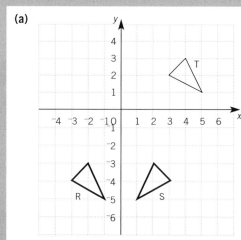

(b) A reflection in the line $y = {}^-x$.

Now try these exam questions:

1
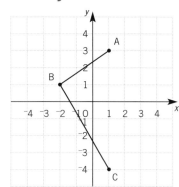

(a) Find the coordinates of the midpoint of $\overrightarrow{AB}$.
(b) Calculate the length of $\overrightarrow{BC}$, showing your working.

2
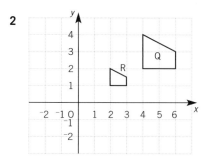

(a) For these quadrilaterals, describe fully the single transformation that maps Q onto R.
(b) Q is reflected in $x = 4$, and then in $y = 1$. Describe fully the single transformation that is equivalent to these two transformations.

3 r, a and b are all lengths. Which of the following expressions could be a volume?

(a) $\dfrac{ar}{2}(4b + \pi r)$ (c) $4a^2b + rb^3$

(b) $2(ab)^2 + \pi r^2 b$ (d) $2abr + \dfrac{\pi ar^2}{2}$

4 We had two similar jugs on the table. One held 1 litre of water. The other held 50 cl of wine. The larger jug was 24 cm high. Calculate the height of the smaller jug.

5 In Xian, China, you can buy solid scale models of the famous Terracotta Warriors. A model 16 cm high weighs 270 grams and has an armour plate of area 9 cm².

(a) Calculate the armour plate area on a similar model of height 24 cm.

(b) Calculate the weight of the same 24 cm model.

6 The diagram shows triangles T_1, T_2 and T_3.

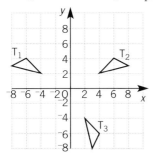

(a) T_2 is a reflection of T_1 in the y-axis. Find the matrix **P** representing the transformation which maps T_1 onto T_2.

(b) T_3 is the image of T_2 under a 90° rotation about the origin. Find the matrix **Q** associated with this transformation.

(c) State the single transformation which is defined by the matrix **QP**.

(d) Explain why the single transformation defined by the matrix **PQ** is not the inverse of the single matrix defined by **QP**.

7 The diagram shows triangles A, B, C and D.

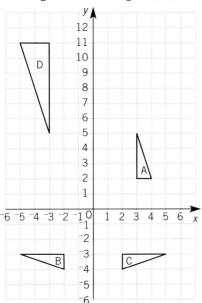

(a) Describe fully the single transformation which maps triangle A onto triangle B.

(b) Find the matrix representing the transformation which maps triangle A onto triangle C.

(c) Triangle A is mapped onto triangle D by an enlargement. Find

  (i) the scale factor of this enlargement

  (ii) the coordinates of the centre of this enlargement.

(d) The matrix $\begin{pmatrix} 2 & 1 \\ 0 & 3 \end{pmatrix}$ represents the transformation which maps triangle A onto triangle E. Find

  (i) the coordinates of the vertices of triangle E

  (ii) the area of triangle E

  (iii) the matrix representing the transformation which maps triangle E onto triangle A.

8 The diagram shows a parallelogram ABCD.

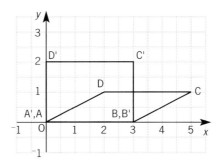

The parallelogram is mapped onto rectangle A'B'C'D' by two consecutive shear transformations.

(a) Describe each shear as fully as possible.

(b) Find the matrix which gives the combined transformation.

9 The rectangle ABCD is transformed into shape by A'B'C'D' by the transformation given by the matrix $\begin{pmatrix} 1 & 1 \\ 0 & 1 \end{pmatrix}$.

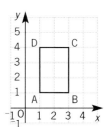

(a) (i) Describe the shape A'B'C'D'.

  (ii) Describe fully the transformation.

(b) Shape A'B'C'D' is transformed by the matrix $\begin{pmatrix} 1 & -1 \\ 0 & 1 \end{pmatrix}$.

  (i) Describe this new shape.

  (ii) Describe fully the transformation.

Vectors

Vectors

- Vectors are added by starting one vector where the previous one finishes.
- To subtract two vectors, use $\mathbf{a} - \mathbf{b} = \mathbf{a} + {}^{-}\mathbf{b}$.
- The resultant of two vectors $\mathbf{a}$ and $\mathbf{b}$ is $\mathbf{a} + \mathbf{b}$.
- If they are in component form, vectors may be added by adding their corresponding components.
- $\mathbf{a} = k\mathbf{b}$ means that $\mathbf{a}$ is parallel to $\mathbf{b}$ and it is k times as long.
- $\overrightarrow{AB} = k\overrightarrow{AC}$ means that A, B and C are in a straight line and the length of $\overrightarrow{AB} = k \times$ the length of $\overrightarrow{AC}$.

Example

$\mathbf{a} = \begin{pmatrix} 3 \\ 4 \end{pmatrix}$, $\mathbf{b} = \begin{pmatrix} 2 \\ -1 \end{pmatrix}$,

$\mathbf{a} + \mathbf{b} = \begin{pmatrix} 5 \\ 3 \end{pmatrix}$

Now try these:

1   $\mathbf{a} = \begin{pmatrix} 2 \\ 5 \end{pmatrix}$ and $\mathbf{b} = \begin{pmatrix} -1 \\ 2 \end{pmatrix}$.

  (a) Find $\mathbf{a} + \mathbf{b}$ and $\mathbf{a} - \mathbf{b}$.
  (b) Calculate the length of $\mathbf{b}$, giving your answer to 3 s.f.

2   Show that the line joining A $(^{-}1, \ ^{-}3)$ and B $(5, 6)$ is parallel to the vector $\begin{pmatrix} 2 \\ 3 \end{pmatrix}$.

3   The position vectors of A, B and C from O are $\mathbf{a}$, $\mathbf{b}$, and $4\mathbf{b} - 3\mathbf{a}$ respectively.

  (a) Find $\overrightarrow{AB}$ in terms of $\mathbf{a}$ and $\mathbf{b}$.
  (b) Show clearly that A, B and C lie in a straight line.

Vector magnitude

- The magnitude of a vector $\mathbf{a}$ or $\overrightarrow{AB}$ is its length and is written as $|\mathbf{a}|$ or $|\overrightarrow{AB}|$.
- To find the magnitude of a vector use Pythagoras' theorem.

Example

Calculate **(a)** $|\mathbf{a}|$ **(b)** $|\overrightarrow{AB}|$.

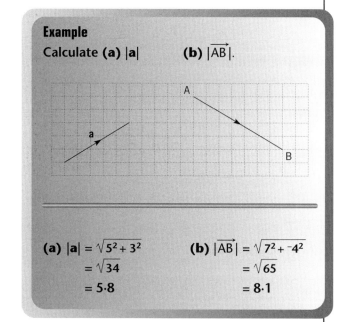

(a) $|\mathbf{a}| = \sqrt{5^2 + 3^2}$
$\phantom{|\mathbf{a}|} = \sqrt{34}$
$\phantom{|\mathbf{a}|} = 5 \cdot 8$

(b) $|\overrightarrow{AB}| = \sqrt{7^2 + {}^{-}4^2}$
$\phantom{|\overrightarrow{AB}|} = \sqrt{65}$
$\phantom{|\overrightarrow{AB}|} = 8 \cdot 1$

Now try these

4 Calculate the magnitude of each of these vectors.

  (a) $\mathbf{x} = \begin{pmatrix} 2 \\ 5 \end{pmatrix}$ (b) $\mathbf{y} = \begin{pmatrix} 3 \\ 4 \end{pmatrix}$ (c) $\mathbf{z} = \begin{pmatrix} 8 \\ -3 \end{pmatrix}$.

5 Calculate the magnitude of each of these vectors.

  (a) $\overrightarrow{AB} = \begin{pmatrix} -3 \\ 7 \end{pmatrix}$ (b) $\overrightarrow{PQ} = \begin{pmatrix} 6 \\ -5 \end{pmatrix}$ (c) $\overrightarrow{XY} = \begin{pmatrix} 3 \\ 2 \end{pmatrix}$.

6 Given the vectors

  $\mathbf{f} = \begin{pmatrix} -3 \\ 4 \end{pmatrix}$, $\mathbf{g} = \begin{pmatrix} 3 \\ -2 \end{pmatrix}$ and $\mathbf{h} = \begin{pmatrix} 5 \\ -3 \end{pmatrix}$,

  calculate the magnitude of
  (a) $\mathbf{f} + \mathbf{h}$ (d) $2\mathbf{g} + 3\mathbf{f}$
  (b) $2\mathbf{g} - \mathbf{f}$ (e) $3\mathbf{h} - 2\mathbf{f}$.
  (c) $\mathbf{g} + \mathbf{h}$

Position vectors

A position vector is a vector in relation to a fixed point.

Now try these:

7 On a suitable grid, plot

(a) A where A has the position vector $\binom{7}{4}$ relative to the origin

(b) B where B has the position vector $\binom{-5}{1}$ relative to A

(c) C where C has the position vector $\binom{-4}{-3}$ relative to B

(d) D where D has the position vector $\binom{2}{-5}$ relative to C

(e) E where E has the position vector $\binom{-4}{-1}$ relative to D

(f) F where F has the position vector $\binom{8}{5}$ relative to E.

8 (a) Write down the position vectors, relative to O, of points A to J.

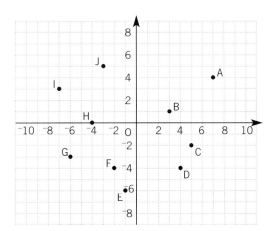

(b) Write down the position vectors of
(i) A relative to H
(ii) B relative to I
(iii) C relative to G
(iv) D relative to H
(v) E relative to A
(vi) F relative to J
(vii) G relative to B
(viii) H relative to C
(ix) I relative to D
(x) J relative to G.

Example
Write down the position vectors, relative to O, of points A to J.

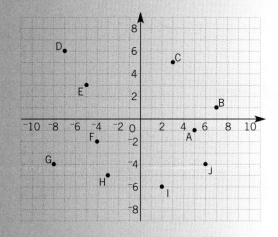

$\overrightarrow{OA} = \binom{5}{-1}$, $\overrightarrow{OB} = \binom{7}{1}$, $\overrightarrow{OC} = \binom{3}{5}$, $\overrightarrow{OD} = \binom{-7}{6}$,

$\overrightarrow{OE} = \binom{-5}{3}$, $\overrightarrow{OF} = \binom{-4}{-2}$, $\overrightarrow{OG} = \binom{-8}{-4}$, $\overrightarrow{OH} = \binom{-3}{-5}$,

$\overrightarrow{OI} = \binom{2}{-6}$, $\overrightarrow{OJ} = \binom{6}{-4}$.

Example
Using the diagram above write down the position vectors of the following.

(a) A relative to E
(b) B relative to H
(c) C relative to G
(d) D relative to A
(e) H relative to E
(f) E relative to C

(a) $\binom{10}{-4}$ (d) $\binom{-12}{7}$

(b) $\binom{10}{6}$ (e) $\binom{2}{-8}$

(c) $\binom{11}{9}$ (f) $\binom{-8}{-2}$

Here is an exam question

...and its solution

(a) (i)

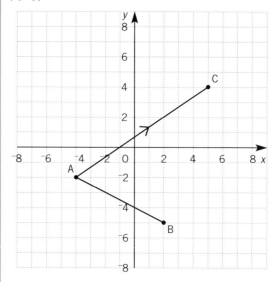

(ii) B = (2, ⁻5)

(iii) $\overrightarrow{BC} = \begin{pmatrix} 3 \\ 9 \end{pmatrix}$.

(b) $|\overrightarrow{BC}| = \sqrt{(3^2 + 9^2)}$

$= \sqrt{90}$

$= 9.5$

Point A is marked on the grid.

$\overrightarrow{AB} = \begin{pmatrix} 6 \\ -3 \end{pmatrix}$ and $\overrightarrow{AC} = \begin{pmatrix} 9 \\ 6 \end{pmatrix}$.

(a) (i)   Copy the grid and draw $\overrightarrow{AB}$ and $\overrightarrow{AC}$ on it.

(ii) Write down the coordinates of B.

(iii) Write down the position vector of C relative to B.

(b) Calculate $|\overrightarrow{BC}|$.

Now try these exam questions:

1   A and C have coordinates (⁻2, 1) and (2, ⁻2)
    respectively. $\overrightarrow{AB} = \begin{pmatrix} 6 \\ 5 \end{pmatrix}$. M is the midpoint of $\overrightarrow{AB}$
    and N is the midpoint of $\overrightarrow{AC}$.

(a) Write down the coordinates of B, M and N.

(b) Calculate the vectors $\overrightarrow{BC}$ and $\overrightarrow{MN}$.

(c) State the relationship between BC and MN.

2

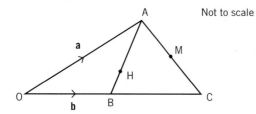

In the diagram $\overrightarrow{OA} = \mathbf{a}$ and $\overrightarrow{OB} = \mathbf{b}$.
M is the midpoint of AC and B is the midpoint of OC.

(a) Write down the following vectors in terms of **a** and
    b, simplifying your answers where possible.

(i) $\overrightarrow{OC}$ (ii) $\overrightarrow{BA}$ (iii) $\overrightarrow{OM}$

(b) H is a point on $\overrightarrow{BA}$ and $\overrightarrow{BH} = \frac{1}{3} \overrightarrow{BA}$. Find the vector
    $\overrightarrow{OH}$ in terms of **a** and **b**.

(c) What do your results tell you about the points
    O, H and M?

3   Draw axes from ⁻8 to 8 for x and ⁻4 to 4 for y.

(a) Plot the points A (⁻7, ⁻1), B (2, 2), C (7, 1) and
    D (3, ⁻3).

(b) Write down the position vector of

(i)   C relative to A

(ii) B relative to D.

(c) Calculate $|\overrightarrow{AC}|$.

4 (a) On a suitable grid, draw a diagram to represent
      these vectors.

(i) $\overrightarrow{OX} = \begin{pmatrix} 7 \\ -2 \end{pmatrix}$ (ii) $\overrightarrow{OY} = \begin{pmatrix} -3 \\ 4 \end{pmatrix}$

(b) Write $\overrightarrow{YX}$ as a column vector.

(c) The quadrilateral OXYZ is a parallelogram.
    Plot point Z on the grid and write down the
    position vector of Z relative to O.

Measures

Changing units

You need to know how to change between the common metric area and volume units.
Here is a list.

Area $1\,cm^2 = 10^2\,mm^2 = 100\,mm^2$
         $1\,m^2 = 100^2\,cm^2 = 10\,000\,cm^2$

Volume $1\,cm^3 = 10^3\,mm^3 = 1000\,mm^3$
         $1\,m^3 = 100^3\,cm^3 = 1\,000\,000\,cm^3$

Capacity   1 litre = 1000 ml $1\,m^3 = 1000$ litres

Now try these:

Change these units.

1 $40\,cm^2$ to mm^2

2 $1 \cdot 50\,m^2$ to cm^2

3 $1 \cdot 5\,m^3$ to litres

4 $5\,254\,000\,cm^3$ to m^3

5 $500\,mm^2$ to cm^2

6 $15 \cdot 3\,cm^3$ to mm^3

7 $6 \cdot 3\,m^3$ to cm^3

8 $24\,000$ litres to m^3

Example

Change these units
(a) $15\,cm^2$ to mm^2
(b) $105\,m^2$ to cm^2
(c) $31\,800\,cm^2$ to m^2
(d) $4 \cdot 2\,cm^3$ to mm^3
(e) $750\,000\,cm^3$ to m^3

(a) $1500\,mm^2$ — × by 100
(b) $1\,050\,000\,cm^2$ — × by 10 000
(c) $3 \cdot 18\,m^2$ — ÷ by 10 000
(d) $4200\,mm^3$ — × by 1000
(e) $0 \cdot 75\,m^3$ — ÷ by 1 000 000

Compound measures

- For speed (s), distance (d) and time (t) you need to know and be able to use
  $s = \frac{d}{t}$, $d = s \times t$ and $t = \frac{d}{s}$.

- For density (D), mass (m) and volume (V) you need to know and be able to use
  $D = \frac{m}{V}$, $m = D \times V$ and $V = \frac{m}{D}$.

- Other compound measures such as population density need to be dealt with separately.

Now try these:

9   Find the distance travelled in $9 \cdot 2$ seconds at $32 \cdot 5\,cm$ per second.

10   Find the volume of a metal ingot which has a mass of $85\,g$ and a density of $16\,g/cm^3$.

11   The population of an island is 437 and the area of the island is $6 \cdot 4\,km^2$. Work out the population density of the island.

Example

Find the speed of a car which travelled 105 km in 2 h 25 min.

The time needs to be changed to hours
$= 2 \cdot 417$ hours
$s = \frac{d}{t} = \frac{105}{2 \cdot 417} = 43 \cdot 44 = 43 \cdot 4$ km/h

4 s.f. should be enough.

Bounds of measurement

- A length measured as $45\,cm$ to the nearest centimetre lies between $44 \cdot 5$ and $45 \cdot 5\,cm$.
  So the bounds are $44 \cdot 5$ and $45 \cdot 5\,cm$.

- A mass measured as $1 \cdot 38\,kg$ correct to 3 s.f. has bounds $1 \cdot 375$ and $1 \cdot 385\,kg$.

- The bounds are always a half unit down and up in the figure after the degree of accuracy.

Example

Give the bounds of these measurements. The accuracy of the measurements is given in brackets.

(a) $80\,cm$ ($10\,cm$)
(b) $8.6\,cm$ (mm)
(c) $48\,g$ (g)
(d) $10 \cdot 5$ second (tenth of a second)
(e) $5 \cdot 23$ litres (3 s.f.)

A very common error is to give the upper bound in (a) as $84 \cdot 999$ and in (b) as $8 \cdot 6499$ etc.

(a) 75 to 85 cm
(b) 8·55 to 8·65 cm
(c) 47·5 to 48·5 g
(d) 10·45 to 10·55 s
(e) 5·225 to 5·235 litres

Now try these:

12 Give the bounds of these measurements. The accuracy is given in brackets.
  (a) 73 g (g) (b) 4·3 litre (0·1 litre) (c) 7·05 m (3 s.f.)

13 Jack won a race in 25·7 seconds. The time was measured to the nearest tenth of a second.
  Between what values must the time lie?

Upper and lower bounds of combined measurements

- To find the upper bound of a sum, add the two upper bounds.
- To find the lower bound of a sum, add the two lower bounds.
- To find the upper bound of a difference, subtract the lower bound from the upper bound.
- To find the lower bound of a difference, subtract the upper bound from the lower bound.
- To find the upper bound of a product, multiply the upper bounds.
- To find the lower bound of a product, multiply the lower bounds.
- To find the upper bound of a division, divide the upper bound by the lower bound.
- To find the lower bound of a division, divide the lower bound by the upper bound.

Now try these:

14 $P = ab - 2c$, $a = 2·1$, $b = 5·4$ and $c = 3·6$ correct to 2 s.f. Find the lower and upper bounds of the value of P.

15 A rectangle has an area of 14·5 cm^2 and a length of 4·6 cm both measured to the nearest 0·1 unit. Work out the limits between which the width must lie.

Example
(a) A rectangle has sides 3·5 cm and 4·6 cm measured to 2 s.f. Find the minimum and maximum value of:
  (i) the perimeter
  (ii) the area.

(b) $A = \frac{3b}{c}$, $b = 3·62$, $c = 5·41$ to 2 d.p.
  Find the lower and upper bounds of A.

(a) (i) Minimum perimeter
  $= 2 \times 3·45 + 2 \times 4·55 = 16$ cm
  Maximum perimeter
  $= 2 \times 3·55 + 2 \times 4·65 = 16·4$ cm
  (ii) Minimum area
  $= 3·45 \times 4·55 = 15·6975 = 15·7$ cm^2
  Maximum area
  $= 3·55 \times 4·65 = 16·5075 = 16·5$ cm^2
(b)
  Lower bound of $A = \frac{3 \times 3·615}{5·415} = 2·0028 = 2·00$
  Upper bound of $A = \frac{3 \times 3·625}{5·405} = 2·0120 = 2·01$

Here is an exam question ...and its solution

When a ball is thrown upwards the maximum height, h, it reaches is given by $h = \frac{U^2}{2g}$.
It is given that $U = 4·2$ and $g = 9·8$ both correct to 2 s.f. Calculate the upper and lower bounds of h.

Now try these exam questions:

1 A pane of glass is 3·5 mm thick and measures 1·4 m by 0·9 m. Work out the volume of the glass:
  (a) in mm^3 (b) in m^3.

2 The volume of a solid metal cylinder is 600 cm^3. The density of the metal is 15 g/cm^3. Calculate the mass of the metal cylinder in kilograms.

3 A formula used in science is $a = \frac{v - u}{t}$.
  $u = 17·4$, $v = 30·3$ and $t = 2·6$, all measured correct to the nearest 0·1. Find the maximum possible value of a.

Upper bound = 0.926 Lower bound = 0.874

To find the upper bound of h, use the upper bound of U and the lower bound of g.
To find the lower bound of h use the opposite.
Upper $h = \frac{4·25^2}{2 \times 9·75} = 0·926282 = 0·926$
Lower $h = \frac{4·15^2}{2 \times 9·85} = 0·8742385 = 0·874$

4 The population of Kenya is $2·6 \times 10^7$, correct to 2 s.f. The area of Kenya is $5·8 \times 10^5$ square kilometres, correct to 2 s.f. Calculate the lower and upper bounds for the population density of Kenya.

5 In 1988 a firm produced 1·2 billion litres of fizzy drink (correct to 2 s.f.). The volume of a standard swimming pool is 390 m^3 (correct to 2 s.f.). What is the greatest number of these swimming pools that could possibly be filled with this amount of fizzy drink?

Constructions

Drawing triangles

You should be able to construct
a triangle given:

- three sides

Example

Step 1: Draw line AB of given
length.
Step 2: Use compasses to
construct arcs AC and
BC with the compasses
set to the given lengths.
Step 3: Draw AC and BC.

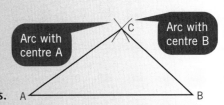

- two sides and the angle
  between them

Example

Step 1: Draw line AB of given length.
Step 2: Measure angle at A.
Step 3: Draw line AC of given length.
Step 4: Join C to B.

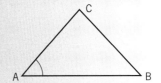

- two angles and one side

Example

Step 1: Draw line AB of given length.
Step 2: Measure angles at A and B.
Step 3: Draw lines AC and BC.

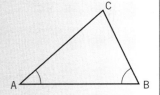

- two sides and an angle.

Example

Step 1: Draw line AB of given length.
Step 2: Measure angle at A.
Step 3: Draw a line from A towards C.
Step 4: To fix C, draw an arc at B, the
radius of the arc being the second
given length.
This construction may give two possible triangles, ABC or ABC'.

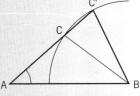

Now try these:

Draw these triangles accurately.
For each triangle measure the length of any unmarked sides and the size of any unknown angles.

1
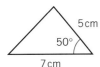

3
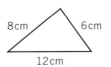

2

4

Angle constructions

You also need to construct, using a ruler and compasses:

- the perpendicular bisector of a line

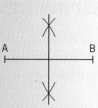

- the bisector of an angle

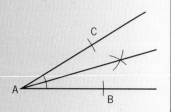

Now try these:

5 Draw this triangle accurately.
  PX is the perpendicular bisector of line AB. AZ is the
  bisector of the angle at A and crosses PX at Z.
  Draw these lines accurately and measure the
  distance AZ.

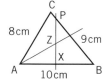

6 Draw, using ruler and compasses only, an equilateral
  triangle, ABC, of side 10 cm.
  Bisect two of the angles as shown, making an
  isosceles triangle, BXC. Measure the 2 equal sides,
  BX and CX of this isosceles triangle.

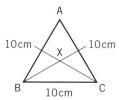

Here is an exam question   ...and its solution

Two buoys are anchored at A and B. A boat is
anchored at C.
Using a scale of 1 cm to
2 m draw the triangle
ABC and measure
the bearing of the
boat, C, from
buoy A.

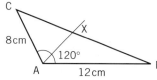

This is a standard construction as shown above:
Draw line AB 7·5 cm long. Using compasses
measure an arc 10 cm from A and 4 cm from B.
Mark the point C where they cross.
Using a protractor measure ∠CAB and subtract
the measurement from 90°. The bearing should
be between 20° and 21°.

Now try these exam questions:

1 The diagram shows a triangle ABC. The bisector of the
  angle at A meets
  line BC at X.
  Construct the triangle
  and measure the
  distance AX.

2 ABC is an equilateral triangle of side
  10 cm. MX is the perpendicular
  bisector of side AB, MY the
  perpendicular bisector of side BC
  and MZ the perpendicular bisector
  of side AC. Draw the triangle and
  measure the distance MZ.

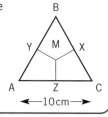

2D shapes

Area formulae and circumference of a circle

You need to know these formulae.

- Rectangle 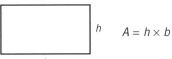 $A = h \times b$

- Triangle $A = \dfrac{b \times h}{2}$

- Parallelogram 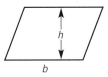 $A = b \times h$

- Trapezium 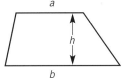 $A = \dfrac{h}{2}(a + b)$

- Circle $A = \pi \times r^2$

- The circumference is another name for the perimeter of a circle.

 $C = \pi \times d$

Example

The corners of a triangle are (2, 1), (2, ⁻3) and (14, ⁻3). Find its area.

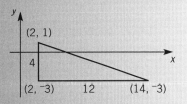

$$A = \frac{12 \times 4}{2} = 24 \text{ units}^2$$

Example

Find the area and perimeter of this shape.

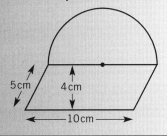

$$A = \frac{1}{2} \times \pi \times 5^2 + 10 \times 4$$
$$= 39 \cdot 3 + 40$$
$$= 79 \cdot 3 \text{ cm}^2$$
$$P = 5 + 10 + 5 + \frac{1}{2} \times \pi \times 10$$
$$= 35 \cdot 7 \text{ cm}$$

Example

A circular pond has an area of 40 m². Find the radius of the pond.

$$A = \pi \times r^2$$
$$40 = \pi \times r^2$$
$$\frac{40}{\pi} = r^2$$
$$r = \sqrt{\frac{40}{\pi}}$$
$$r = 3 \cdot 57 \text{ cm}$$

Now try these:

1 Find the area of this shape.

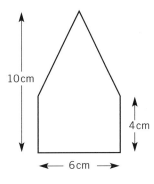

2 A semi-circular rug has a radius of 0·7 m. Calculate the area of the rug.

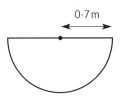

3 A circular path has an internal radius of 8 m and an external radius of 12 m. Find the area of the path.

Arc length and area of a sector of a circle

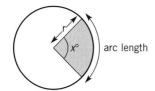

- Arc length = $\frac{x}{360} \times 2\pi r$

- Area of a sector = $\frac{x}{360} \times \pi r^2$

Now try these:

4 A sector of a circle of radius 5 cm has an area of 25 cm². Find the angle at the centre of the circle.

5 AB and CD are arcs of circles centre O. Find the perimeter ABCD of the shaded region.

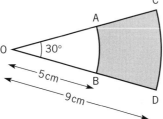

Example

(a) Find the arc length AB.
(b) Find the shaded area.

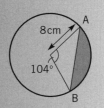

This is known as a segment of the circle.

(a) Arc length = $\frac{104}{360} \times \pi \times 16 = 14 \cdot 5$ cm

(b) Segment = Sector – Triangle
$$= \frac{104}{360} \times \pi \times 8^2 - \frac{1}{2} \times 8 \times 8 \times \sin 104°$$
$$= 27 \cdot 0 \text{ cm}^2$$

Here is an exam question   ...and its solution

A heart shape is made from a square and two semi-circles. Find the area and perimeter of the heart shape.

| $A = 714 \cdot 2$ cm² | $2\left(\frac{1}{2} \times \pi \times 10^2\right) + 20 \times 20$ |
| $P = 102 \cdot 8$ cm | $2\left(\frac{1}{2} \times \pi \times 20\right) + 20 + 20$ |

Now try these exam questions:

1 Find the total area of this shape.

4 A rectangular garden contains eight identical triangular flower beds. The rest of the garden is paths. Work out the total area of the paths.

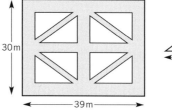

2 The Earth is a sphere. It has a circumference of 40 200 km. Work out the radius of the Earth.

3 Work out the area of the lawn in this diagram.

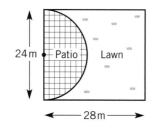

5 The diagram shows a tunnel entrance. The roof of the tunnel is part of a circle, centre O and radius 14·5 m. Calculate the area of cross-section of the tunnel.

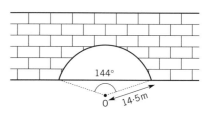

Loci

Basic loci

- A locus is a path or region where a point can move according to a rule.

- The locus of a point which moves so it is 3 cm from a fixed point A is a circle, centre A, radius 3 cm.

- The locus of a point which moves so it is less than 3 cm from a fixed point A is the region inside a circle, centre A, radius 3 cm.

- The locus of a point which moves so it is more than 3 cm from a fixed point A is the region outside a circle, centre A, radius 3 cm.

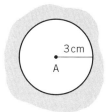

- The locus of a point which stays 2 cm from a fixed straight line is one of a pair of lines parallel to that line.

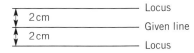

- The locus of a point which stays an equal distance from two fixed points is the perpendicular bisector of the line joining the two points.

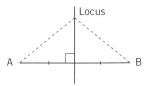

- The locus of a point which stays an equal distance from two fixed lines is one or both of the angle bisectors of the lines.

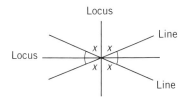

Example

A goat is tethered by a 2 m rope to a rail 3 m long fixed in a field of grass. Draw a scale diagram to show the region of grass which the goat can eat.

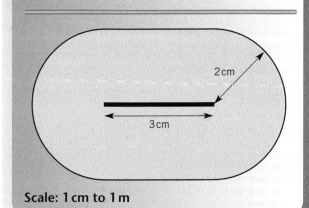

Scale: 1 cm to 1 m

Now try these:

Draw accurately the locus for each of the following.

1 A point moves so it is 4 cm from a fixed point P.

2 A and B are fixed points 6.5 cm apart.
   (a) Draw the locus of points which are equidistant from A and B.
   (b) Shade the locus of points which are nearer A than B.

3 Two sides of a field meet at an angle of 70°. A footpath starts from this corner of the field and goes across the field keeping the same distance from each side of the field. Draw the footpath.

4 A stretch of coast has the shoreline running south-east to north-west. A boat moves keeping 500 m from this shore. Draw a scale diagram to show its path.

Problems involving intersecting loci

Often, exam questions involve more than one locus. Solve these questions in stages, drawing one locus at a time.

If the question does not tell you which to shade, you may shade the required region or those not required. Shading those not required is often easier if there are several loci. Remember to give a key or label the diagram to make it clear which you have done.

Here is an exam question ...and its solution

This is the plan of a garden drawn on a scale of 1 cm to 2 m. A pond is to be dug in the garden.

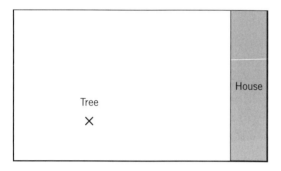

It must be at least 4 m from the tree. It must be at least 3 m from the house.

Shade the region where the pond could be dug.

Show all your construction lines.

Scale 1 cm to 2 m

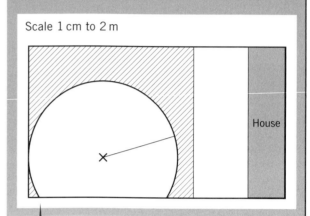

At least 4 m from the tree – so outside a circle radius 2 cm centre the tree.
At least 3 m from the house, so to the left of a line parallel to the house and 1·5 cm from it.

Now try these exam questions:

1 Ashwell and Buxbourne are two towns, 50 km apart. Chris is house hunting. He has decided he would like to live closer to Buxbourne than Ashwell but no further than 30 km from Ashwell.
Using a scale of 1 cm to represent 5 km, shade the area in which Chris should look for a house.

2 Ashad's garden is a rectangle. He is deciding where to plant a new apple tree. It must be nearer to the hedge AB than the house CD. It must be at least 2 m from fences AC and BD. It must be more than 6 m from corner A.
Shade the region where the tree can be planted.
Leave in all your construction lines.
Make the scale of your drawing 1 cm to 2 m.

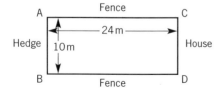

3 Sandtown council wants to build a pavilion on a playing field. They decide to site it at an equal distance from both gates and not more than 250 m from the toilet block.
On a scale drawing, make suitable constructions to locate the site. Leave in your construction lines. Show clearly where the pavilion can be built.
Scale: 1 cm represents 50 m.

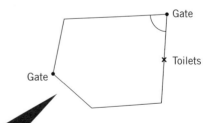

To answer this question, draw a pentagon of about this shape, with the gates 13·2 cm apart and the toilet block 4·5 cm from one gate. The angle at the top, as indicated, is 82°.

Processing and representing data

Statistics and probability

Frequency polygons

A frequency polygon is formed by joining, with straight lines, the midpoints of the tops of the bars in a frequency diagram.

Example

The table shows the amounts of pocket money received by the members of a class.

Amount ($)	0– 3·99	4–7·99	8–11·99	12–15·99
Frequency	3	10	12	5

Draw a frequency polygon.

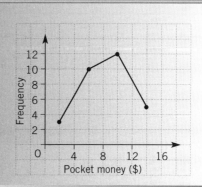

Histograms

- Histograms are particularly useful when you are dealing with unequal intervals.
- A histogram is similar to a frequency diagram except that on a histogram the area of the bar is equal to the frequency.
  - Width of interval × height of bar = frequency
  - Height = $\dfrac{\text{frequency}}{\text{width of interval}}$
- The height is called the frequency density.

Example

The table below shows the distribution of times (t minutes) that a company took to answer 100 telephone calls.

Time (t minutes)	Frequency (f)	Frequency density = $f \div$ width
$0 < t \leqslant 2$	28	
$2 < t \leqslant 5$	48	
$5 < t \leqslant 10$	12	
$10 < t \leqslant 15$	7	
$15 < t \leqslant 20$	5	

(a) Complete the column for frequency density.
(b) Draw a histogram to represent the data.

(a) Frequency densities: 14, 16, 2·4, 1·4, 1.
(b)

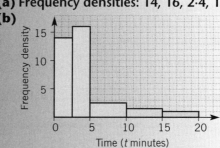

s_
____
39780340815786

Now try these:

1 The distribution of the masses (*m* kg) of 200 parcels received at a parcel sorting office are shown in the table below.

Mass (*m* kg)	Frequency (*f*)	Frequency density = *f* ÷ width
$0 < m \leqslant 0.5$	21	
$0.5 < m \leqslant 1$	33	
$1 < m \leqslant 2$	55	
$2 < m \leqslant 5$	45	
$5 < m \leqslant 10$	30	
$10 < m \leqslant 20$	16	

(a) Copy the table and complete the column for frequency density.

(b) Draw a histogram to represent the data.

2 The table below shows the distribution of heights (*h* cm) of 120 plants.

Height (*h* cm)	Frequency (*f*)	Frequency density = *f* ÷ width
$0 < h \leqslant 5$	8	
$5 < h \leqslant 10$	20	
$10 < h \leqslant 20$	50	
$20 < h \leqslant 30$	25	
$30 < h \leqslant 50$	17	

(a) Copy the table and complete the column for frequency density.

(b) Draw a histogram to represent the data.

(c) Calculate the mean height of the plants.

Mean from a frequency distribution

- To calculate the mean from a frequency distribution for grouped data:

  1 Use the middle of the interval for the value of *x*.
  2 Multiply each observation (*x*) by its corresponding frequency.
  3 Add up these results.
  4 Divide by the total frequency.

  > You are often told the total frequency in the question.

Example

Find the mean amount of pocket money received by the students in the class in the first example.

Mid-interval value (*x*)	2	6	10	14
Frequency	3	10	12	5

$$\text{Mean} = \frac{2 \times 3 + 6 \times 10 + 10 \times 12 + 14 \times 5}{3 + 10 + 12 + 5}$$

$$= 256 \div 30 = \$8.53$$

Now try these:

3 The distribution of the lengths (ℓ cm) of 100 oak tree leaves are shown in the following frequency table.

ℓ (cm)	*f*
$8 \leqslant \ell < 9$	8
$9 \leqslant \ell < 10$	18
$10 \leqslant \ell < 11$	35
$11 \leqslant \ell < 12$	23
$12 \leqslant \ell < 13$	16

For this information:

(a) draw a frequency polygon

(b) find the mean length.

4 The table below shows the heights of 100 basketball players.

Height (*h* cm)	Frequency (*f*)
$160 < h \leqslant 170$	6
$170 < h \leqslant 180$	19
$180 < h \leqslant 190$	41
$190 < h \leqslant 200$	25
$200 < h \leqslant 210$	9

For this information:

(a) draw a frequency polygon

(b) find the mean height.

Cumulative frequency graphs

- Cumulative frequency is the running total of the frequencies in a distribution. The last cumulative frequency is the total of the frequencies and is often given in the question.

- Cumulative frequency is plotted at the upper bound of each interval. The points can be joined by a curve or by straight lines. The graph opposite shows a fairly typical shape for a cumulative frequency curve.

- To find the median of a frequency distribution draw a line across the graph at half the total frequency to meet the curve and then down to read off the value on the x-axis.

- To find the quartiles of a frequency distribution draw lines across the graph at a quarter and three quarters of the total frequency to meet the curve and then down to read off the values on the x-axis.

- Interquartile range (upper quartile – lower quartile) is a measure of spread.

Now try these:

5 The table shows the results of a survey on the times (t minutes) taken by 100 students to get to school.

Time (t minutes)	Frequency
$0 < t \leqslant 10$	8
$10 < t \leqslant 20$	15
$20 < t \leqslant 30$	33
$30 < t \leqslant 40$	22
$40 < t \leqslant 50$	17
$50 < t \leqslant 60$	5

(a) Draw up a table of cumulative frequencies.
(b) Draw a cumulative frequency graph.
(c) Use your graph to find:
   (i) the number of students who took over 45 minutes to get to school
   (ii) the median time
   (iii) the interquartile range.

6 The cumulative frequency graph opposite shows the marks obtained by 120 students in their last Maths exam.
   (a) The pass mark was 45. How many passed?
   (b) Find the median and interquartile range.

Example

The table below shows the distribution of the masses (mg) of 80 tomatoes.
(a) Complete the right-hand column to show the cumulative frequencies.
(b) Draw a cumulative frequency diagram.
(c) Estimate the number of tomatoes weighing more than 93 g.
(d) Find the median and interquartile range.

Mass (g)	Frequency	Cumulative frequency (a)
$70 < m \leqslant 75$	4	4
$75 < m \leqslant 80$	10	14
$80 < m \leqslant 85$	22	36
$85 < m \leqslant 90$	27	63
$90 < m \leqslant 95$	14	77
$95 < m \leqslant 100$	3	80

(b)

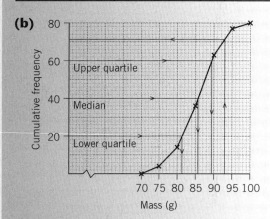

(c) $80 - 71 = 9$
(d) Median = 86 g
   Interquartile range = $89{\cdot}5 - 81{\cdot}5 = 8$ g.

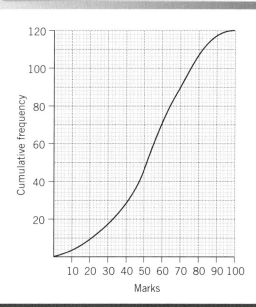

Here is an exam question

...and its solution

A test was carried out to establish the ability of a mouse to find food. The test was carried out on 120 mice. The distribution of times taken to reach the food is given in the table below.

Time (*t* seconds)	Frequency
$0 < t \leqslant 10$	18
$10 < t \leqslant 15$	46
$15 < t \leqslant 20$	35
$20 < t \leqslant 30$	13
$30 < t \leqslant 50$	8

Draw a histogram to represent this information.

Now try these exam questions:

1 The weight in kilograms of each of 80 children under 10 in a village is summarised in the table below.

Weight (*w* kilograms)	Frequency
$0 < w \leqslant 5$	9
$5 < w \leqslant 10$	13
$10 < w \leqslant 15$	21
$15 < w \leqslant 20$	17
$20 < w \leqslant 25$	10
$25 < w \leqslant 30$	8
$30 < w \leqslant 35$	2

(a) (i) Copy and complete the cumulative frequency table.

Weight (*w* kilograms)	Cumulative frequency
$w \leqslant 5$	9
$w \leqslant 10$	
$w \leqslant 15$	
$w \leqslant 20$	
$w \leqslant 25$	
$w \leqslant 30$	
$w \leqslant 35$	

(ii) Draw the cumulative frequency graph for the weight of the children. Use a scale of 2 cm to 5 kg on the horizontal axis and 1 cm to 10 children on the vertical axis.

Time (*t* seconds)	Frequency	Frequency density
$0 < t \leqslant 10$	18	1·8
$10 < t \leqslant 15$	46	9·2
$15 < t \leqslant 20$	35	7
$20 < t \leqslant 30$	13	1·3
$30 < t \leqslant 50$	8	0·4

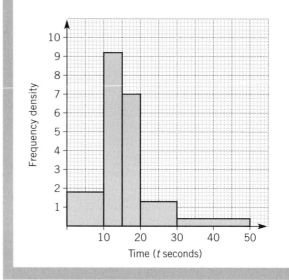

(b) Use your graph to find:
   (i) the median weight
   (ii) the interquartile range.
(c) Use your graph to estimate how many children weigh at least 8 kg.

2 150 apples were picked and weighed. Their weights are shown in the table below.

Weight (*w* grams)	Number of apples	Mid-interval value	
$50 < w \leqslant 60$	23	55	
$60 < w \leqslant 70$	42		
$70 < w \leqslant 80$	50		
$80 < w \leqslant 90$	20		
$90 < w \leqslant 100$	15		

Calculate an estimate of the mean weight of an apple.

3 Gary recorded the playing times of each track in his CD collection. The table shows the grouped distribution times.

Time (t minutes)	$1 < t \leqslant 2$	$2 < t \leqslant 3$	$3 < t \leqslant 4$	$4 < t \leqslant 5$	$5 < t \leqslant 6$	$6 < t \leqslant 7$
Number of tracks (frequency)	5	25	45	82	33	10

(a) (i) Write down the modal class.
    (ii) Draw a frequency polygon to represent the distribution. Use a scale of 2 cm to 1 minute on the horizontal axis and 2 cm to 10 tracks on the vertical axis.

(b) Calculate an estimate of the mean playing time of a CD track.

(c) (i) Copy and complete the cumulative frequency table below.

Time (t minutes)	$t \leqslant 1$	$t \leqslant 2$	$t \leqslant 3$	$t \leqslant 4$	$t \leqslant 5$	$t \leqslant 6$	$t \leqslant 7$
Number of tracks	0	5					200

    (ii) Draw the cumulative frequency curve showing the playing times of the CD tracks. Use a scale of 2 cm to 1 minute on the horizontal axis and 2 cm to 50 tracks on the vertical axis.

(d) Use the cumulative frequency curve to estimate:
    (i) the median playing time of a CD track.
    (ii) the probability that a randomly chosen track plays for longer than 3·7 minutes.

4 A doctor's patients are divided by ages as shown in the table below.

Age (x) in years	$0 \leqslant x < 5$	$5 \leqslant x < 15$	$15 \leqslant x < 25$	$25 \leqslant x < 45$	$45 \leqslant x < 75$
Number of calls	14	41	59	70	16

Draw a histogram to represent this information.
Use a scale of 2 cm to 10 years on the x-axis and an area of 1 cm² to represent five patients.

5 A sample was taken of the telephone calls to a school switchboard. The lengths of the telephone calls are recorded, in minutes, in this table.

Time in minutes (t)	$0 < t \leqslant 1$	$1 < t \leqslant 3$	$3 < t \leqslant 5$	$5 < t \leqslant 10$	$10 \leqslant t \leqslant 20$
Number of calls	12	32	19	20	15

Copy and complete the histogram to show this information.

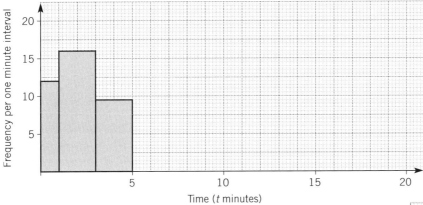

6 All the pupils in a small secondary school were asked how long, on average, they spent each night completing their homework. The results are shown in the histogram opposite.

Copy and complete the following table of frequencies.

Time (minutes)	0–20	20–30	30–45	45–60	60–90
Frequency		60			

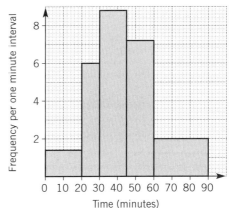

Probability

Basic probability

- Probability can be expressed as fractions, decimals or percentages. All probabilities are between 0 and 1 inclusive.
- P(A doesn't happen) = 1 – P(A)
- For equally likely outcomes,

$$P(A) = \frac{\text{number of ways A can happen}}{\text{total possible number of outcomes}}$$

> Never write probabilities as '1 in 5' or as a ratio '1 to 5' or 1 : 5. You will lose marks if you do. Instead, write $\frac{1}{5}$ or 0·2 (or 20% if the question uses percentages).

> P(A) is a useful shorthand for the probability that A happens.

- **Mutually exclusive** outcomes are those which cannot happen together. If A, B and C are mutually exclusive outcomes covering all the possibilities, then P(A) + P(B) + P(C) = 1.

> **Example**
> If a bag contains just red, green and white balls and one is drawn out at random, what will P(red) + P(green) + P(white) equal?
>
> 1

Relative frequency

$$\text{Relative frequency} = \frac{\text{number of times event occurs}}{\text{total number of trials}}$$

- When theoretical probabilities are not known, relative frequency can be used to estimate probability.
- The greater the number of trials, the better the estimate. The graph of relative frequency against the number of trials may vary greatly at first, but later settles down.
- Relative frequency experiments may be used to test for bias e.g. to see if a dice is fair.

> **Example**
> Sarah experiments with a biased dice. This graph shows the relative frequency of throwing a six, when Sarah threw her dice 1000 times.
>
>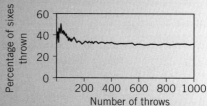
>
> What is the probability of getting a six with this dice?
>
> P(6) = 30% approx.

Now try these:

1 These are the results of 500 spins with a spinner.

No. on spinner	1	2	3	4	5
Frequency	106	92	74	127	101

Find as a decimal the relative frequency of scoring three with this spinner.
Do these results suggest the spinner is biased?
Explain your answer.

2 250 people were asked their favourite colour from a packet of sweets.
24 said mauve, 52 said yellow, 15 said brown, 72 said red and 44 said green.
The other colour was orange.

   (a) How many said orange?
   (b) Estimate the probability that the next person asked says red.

Combining probabilities

- Equally likely outcomes may be listed in a table or shown on a grid.

> Be systematic to make sure you don't miss out any possibilities.

- When outcomes are not equally likely, use **tree diagrams**. Remember:
  - each set of branches shows the possible outcomes of the event
  - the probabilities on each set of branches should add to 1
  - when events are **independent**, the outcomes of the second event are not affected by the outcomes of the first
  - to find the probabilities of the combined events, multiply the probabilities along the branches.

Example

This shows the probabilities that Penny has to stop at lights or a crossing on her way to work.

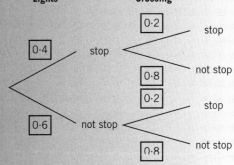

What is the probability that she does not stop at either?

P(not stop at either) = 0·6 × 0·8 = 0·48

Now try these:

3 Jill offers her guests shepherd's pie or macaroni cheese for main course, and blackcurrant cheesecake, chocolate gateau or trifle for dessert.
List the possible two-course meals her guests can have.

4 Draw a grid, with axes marked from 1 to 4, to show the possible outcomes when a fair spinner numbered 1 to 4 is spun twice.
What is the probability of:
(a) getting 1 both times
(b) getting a total of 6?

5 A bakery makes doughnuts. Machine A fills them with jam.
There is a probability of 0·03 that machine A misses a doughnut.
Machine B covers them with sugar.
The probability that machine B misses a doughnut is 0·02.
(a) Draw a tree diagram to show these probabilities, using the first set of branches for machine A.
(b) Calculate the probability that a doughnut has no jam inside and no sugar.
(c) Calculate the probability that a doughnut has just one of these faults.

6 Bob experiments with a biased dice. The probability that it shows a six is $\frac{2}{5}$.
Find the probability that, when the dice is thrown three times, there will be:
(a) three sixes
(b) no sixes
(c) just one six.

> Even if it is not requested, it is a good idea to draw a tree diagram.

Conditional probabilities

- When events are not independent, the outcome of one affects the probability that the other happens.

- In a tree diagram in this case, the probabilities on the second pairs of branches will be different.

> Remember that the sum of the probabilities of all the outcomes is 1.

Example

The probability that Pali wakes up late on a work morning is 0·1. When he wakes up late, the probability that he misses the bus is 0·8. When he doesn't wake up late, the probability that he misses the bus is 0·2. Draw a tree diagram to represent this, and find the probability that he misses the bus on a work morning.

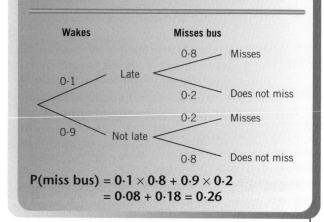

P(miss bus) = 0·1 × 0·8 + 0·9 × 0·2
            = 0·08 + 0·18 = 0·26

Now try these:

7   A bag contains five white, two orange and three black beads.
    A bead is selected at random and its colour noted. It is not replaced.
    A second bead is then selected. Calculate the probability that the two beads are:
    (a) both black
    (b) different colours.

8   A motorist has to go through two sets of traffic lights on her way to work.
    The probability that she has to stop at the first set of lights is $\frac{2}{5}$.
    If she stops at the first set of lights, the probability that she has to stop at the second set is $\frac{3}{4}$.
    If she does not stop at the first set of lights, the probability that she has to stop at the second set is $\frac{1}{10}$.
    On any particular day, what is the probability that:
    (a) she has to stop at just one set of lights on her way to work
    (b) she has to stop at **least** once at the traffic lights on her way to work?

9   On any morning, the probability that I leave home late is $\frac{1}{3}$.
    If I leave late, the probability that I arrive late for work is $\frac{4}{5}$.
    If I leave on time, the probability that I arrive late is $\frac{2}{5}$.
    What is the probability that I shall be late for work tomorrow?

10 There are 15 pens in a box. Five are red and ten green.
    Without looking, I take a pen from the box and do not replace it. I do this twice.
    What is the probability that the pens are different colours?

Here is an exam question   ...and its solution

Pete likes crisps. Without looking, he picks a bag out of an assorted pack. There are 12 bags of crisps in the pack. Two of these bags are ready-salted. The manufacturers say that one bag in every 100 has a gold reward in it. This is independent of the flavour of the crisps.

(a) Complete the tree diagram to show the probabilities.

(b) What is the probability that Pete picks a ready-salted bag with a gold reward in it?

(c) What is the probability that Pete picks either a ready-salted bag or one with a gold reward in it but not both of these?

(a)

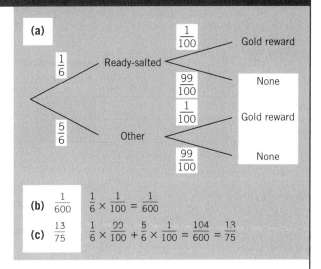

(b) $\frac{1}{600}$ $\frac{1}{6} \times \frac{1}{100} = \frac{1}{600}$

(c) $\frac{13}{75}$ $\frac{1}{6} \times \frac{99}{100} + \frac{5}{6} \times \frac{1}{100} = \frac{104}{600} = \frac{13}{75}$

Now try these exam questions:

1 Ellen and Schweta are practising goal scoring in football. When they each take one shot the probability that Ellen scores a goal is 0·7 and the probability that Schweta scores a goal is 0·8. These probabilities are independent.
   (a) Complete the tree diagram.

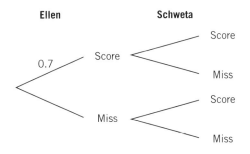

    (b) Calculate the probability that, at their next attempt:
      (i) both Ellen and Schweta score a goal
      (ii) either Ellen or Schweta, but not both, score a goal.

2 Carlotta and Vimal are both members of a walking club. Carlotta goes to 60% of the club's meetings. If Carlotta goes to a meeting, the probability that Vimal will go is $\frac{2}{3}$. If Carlotta does not go to a meeting, the probability that Vimal will go is $\frac{1}{4}$.
   (a) Use this information to complete this tree diagram.

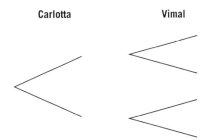

    (b) Using this tree diagram, find the probability that, for a randomly chosen meeting:
      (i) both Carlotta and Vimal will go
      (ii) neither of them will go.

3 James keeps his socks separately in a drawer. The drawer contains four red socks, five white socks and six black socks. He dresses in the dark one morning and pulls out two socks without being able to see their colour.
   What is the probability that he takes:
   (a) two black socks
   (b) two socks of the same colour
   (c) two socks of different colours?

4 **(a)** Jake conducts an experiment with a fair six-sided ordinary dice. He throws it twice. What is the probability that he throws a six both times?
   (b) He throws the dice n times.
   Write down an expression in terms of n for the probability that:
      (i) he does not get a six on any throw
      (ii) he throws at least one six.

5 Box A contains pens. 20% are red, 50% are blue and 30% are black. Box B contains pencils. 15% are blue, 50% are red and 35% are black. Jack takes a pen from Box A and a pencil from Box B at random.
   (a) Draw a tree diagram to show the possible outcomes.
   (b) Work out the probability that he takes a red pen and a red pencil.
   (c) Work out the probability that he takes a pen and pencil of the same colour.

Answers

For full model answers to the exam questions, go to http://www.hoddermaths.co.uk.

Integers

Practice questions (pages 2–3)

1 (a) 4, 8, 12, 16, 20, 24
   (b) 9, 18, 27, 36, 45, 54
   (c) 15, 30, 45, 60, 75, 90
2 (a) 1, 2, 3, 4, 6, 8, 12, 24
   (b) 1, 2, 4, 5, 8, 10, 20, 40
   (c) 1, 2, 4, 8, 16, 32
3 (a) $2 \times 2 \times 3 \times 3$
   (b) $2 \times 2 \times 5 \times 7$
   (c) $2 \times 2 \times 3 \times 7$
4 (a) HCF = 3   LCM = 120
   (b) HCF = 4   LCM = 120
   (c) HCF = 18   LCM = 540
5 (a) $\frac{1}{5}$ (c) $1\frac{1}{3}$ (e) 0·4
   (b) 9   (d) 5
6 (a) 2   (d) 11   (g) $^-4$
   (b) $^-1$ (e) $^-15$ (h) 24
   (c) $^-16$ (f) 4

Exam questions (page 3)

1 (a) 14
   (b) 12 or 18
   (c) 11, 13, 17 or 19
2 $264 = 2 \times 2 \times 2 \times 3 \times 11$
3 HCF = 4   LCM = 48
4 HCF = 2   LCM = 60
5 1
6 13

Powers and roots

Practice questions (pages 4–5)

1   81
2   1
3   $\frac{1}{9}$
4   1
5   216
6   $\frac{1}{8}$
7   (a) 336·0
    (b) 0·174
    (c) $657.97
    (d) 29%
8   5^{10}
9   6^3
10 $8a^9$
11 $6a^2b^{-1}$ or $\frac{6a^2}{b}$
12 c^{10}
13 $8x^{12}$
14 6
15 0·1
16 20·1
17 0·0625
18 372 000
19 0·000 48
20 $5 \cdot 83 \times 10^{-5}$
21 $7 \cdot 56 \times 10^7$
22 $1 \cdot 2 \times 10^{14}$
23 $2 \cdot 5 \times 10^{10}$

Exam questions (page 5)

1 (a) $\frac{1}{81}$ (b) 1   (c) 3
2 (a) (i) 1   (ii) 3   (b) $2 \cdot 4 \times 10^4$
3 (a) $\frac{1}{2}$ (b) p^3q^{-1} or $\frac{p^3}{q}$
4 (a) $8pq^3$ (b) $\frac{8}{343}$
5 (a) $1 \cdot 8 \times 10^8$ (b) $1 \cdot 2 \times 10^{-4}$
6 $8 \cdot 75 \times 10^{-3}$
7 30·2 litres

Fractions and decimals

Practice questions (pages 6–7)

1   $5\frac{13}{24}$
2   $5\frac{7}{15}$
3   $1\frac{11}{20}$
4   $1\frac{1}{12}$
5   $2\frac{17}{30}$
6   $\frac{23}{24}$
7   $10\frac{1}{2}$
8   4
9   $11\frac{2}{5}$
10 $3\frac{1}{3}$
11 $6\frac{2}{3}$
12 $1\frac{4}{5}$
13 25
14 9
15 $28
16 $190
17 $214
18 $1785
19 $\frac{7}{9}$
20 $\frac{61}{99}$
21 $\frac{5}{12}$

Exam questions (page 7)

1 (a) $3\frac{1}{8}$ (b) $1\frac{1}{6}$
2 (a) $3\frac{5}{9}$ (b) $3\frac{17}{20}$
3 (a) $22   (b) $90
4 (a) $\frac{7}{8}$ (b) $1\frac{1}{4}$
5 $h = \frac{1}{3}$
6 (a) $\frac{14}{99}$
   (b) (i)   Recurring. Prime factor of 7.
        (ii) Terminating. Prime factors of 2 and 5.
        (iii) Recurring. Prime factors of 2 and 3.
        (iv) Recurring. Prime factor of 3.
7 18 460

Percentages and ratios

Practice questions (pages 8–9)

1 (a) $89·88
   (b) $6457·50
2 (a) $10·80
   (b) $5723
3 $1714·75
4 $191 896·50
5 60
6 $8200
7 $1200
8 $8120
9 (a) (i)   1 : 3
        (ii) 8 : 3
        (iii) 1 : 5
        (iv) 2 : 5
   (b) (i)   1 : 3
        (ii) 1 : 0·375
        (iii) 1 : 5
        (iv) 1 : 2·5
10 $8, $10
11 21 litres
12 $29·50, $59, $88·50

Exam questions (page 9)

1 (a) $629·30   (b) After four years = $215·8499.
                       A quarter = $224·75.
2 $80
3 $133 300
4 (a) $763·75   (b) 14·9%
5 (a) 100 ml   (b) 300 litres
6 (a) 17·5 cm   (b) 1 : 40 000
7 (a) 70%   (b) 140 men and 160 women.

Answers

Mental methods

Practice questions (pages 10–11)

1. (a) 12
   (b) 0·5
   (c) $\frac{1}{36}$
   (d) $\frac{1}{9}$
   (e) 1
2. $4^{-2}\ 4^0\ 4^{\frac{1}{3}}\ 4^{\frac{1}{2}}\ 4^2$
3. (a) 5·4
   (b) 12
   (c) 0·31
   (d) 45 000
4. (a) 20
   (b) 100
   (c) 0·7
   (d) 1

5. (a) $4·6 \times 10^4$
   (b) $4·84 \times 10^{-2}$
   (c) $3·6 \times 10^6$
   (d) $5·965 \times 10^3$
6. (a) 8 000 000
   (b) 9400
   (c) 77
   (d) 0·000 303
7. 3×10^{-13}
8. $2·4 \times 10^5$
9. 5×10^{10}
10. 4×10^{-1} or 0·4

Exam questions (page 11)

1. 750
2. (a) 2^{11}
   (b) $2·05 \times 10^3$
3. $2·4 \times 10^{10}$
4. 128
5. $5·236 \times 10^{12}$ m

Written methods

Practice questions (pages 12–13)

1. (a) $1\frac{1}{7}$
   (b) $1\frac{3}{8}$
   (c) 1·07
   (d) 1·32
   (e) 1·175
2. (a) $\frac{6}{7}$
   (b) $\frac{5}{8}$
   (c) 0·93
   (d) 0·68
   (e) 0·825
3. 179·2 cm^3
4. 31 888
5. (a) $2185·45
   (b) $2687·83
6. $4331·93

7. $3145·73
8. 11 975
9. (a) 0·5 hrs
   (b) 4 hrs
   (c) 5 hrs
10. (a) $t = \frac{40}{b}$
    (b) 3 hrs 20 mins
    (c) 5
11. (a) $m = 3r^3$
    (b) 375 g
    (c) 4 cm
12. (a) $y = 4\sqrt{x}$
    (b) 12
    (c) 625

Exam questions (page 14)

1. $535·96
2. $172·82
3. $T = 0·2\sqrt{L}$
4. (a) $S = 0·0375L^3$
   (b) 8·1 cm
   (c) 2 m
5. $P = \frac{84}{\sqrt{Q}}$

Calculator methods

Practice questions (pages 15–16)

1. (a) $^-$10   (b) $^-$9   (c) $^-7\frac{1}{2}$ (d) 36   (e) 12   (f) $^-$4
2. (a) $\frac{4}{7}$ (b) $\frac{7}{9}$ (c) $\frac{31}{42}$
3. (a) $1\frac{7}{15}$ (b) $2\frac{7}{12}$ (c) $5\frac{1}{16}$ (d) $1\frac{1}{9}$
4. (a) $93   (b) 20
5. (a) $\frac{1}{8}$ (b) 1·25   (c) 25   (d) $\frac{4}{11}$

6. (a) 625   (b) $^-$2800   (c) 3   (d) 3   (e) 1×10^{-5}
7. (a) 43·35   (b) 8·04   (c) 25·26   (d) 4·00
8. (a) $7·31 \times 10^{-5}$ (b) $1·37 \times 10^{11}$ (c) 4×10^6
9. (a) 2·5   (b) 25·39   (c) 23·87

Exam questions (page 16)

1. (a) 120 g
   (b) $\frac{19}{20}$ or 0·95
   (c) $15·20
2. $\frac{1}{9}$
3. (a) 3·49
   (b) 0·088
   (c) 14·64
4. (a) 831·08
   (b) 5·36
5. (a) $6·43 \times 10^{10}$
   (b) $1·13 \times 10^{32}$
6. (a) 8·07
   (b) 1·08
7. 256

Solving problems

Practice questions (pages 17–18)

1. $16, $24, $32
2. $467·70
3. $16 500
4. 60 km/h
5. 19·3 g/cm^3
6. 220 000 to 3 s.f.
7. (a) $800 \div 20 = 40$
   (b) $\frac{6000}{60 \times 20} = 5$
8. (a) 30·97
   (b) 4·14
   (c) 24·60
9. (a) 5350
   (b) 61·4
   (c) 3050
10. 3·7 and 8·7 (or $^-$3·7 and $^-$8·7)

Exam questions (page 18)

1. (a) $24·50
   (b) $7·32
2. (a) $4900·17
   (b) 8 years
3. 45 km/h
4. (a) $4·5 \times 10^7$
   (b) 120
5. $750
6. 44·9 cm to 1 d.p.

Symbols, indices, factors and expansions

Practice questions (pages 19–21)

1. $4x + 8 = 40$ Width = 8 cm, length = 12 cm.
2. $2x + 10 = 58$ Women = 24, men = 34.
3. $x^2 + 8 = 89$ Number = ±9.
4. $8a^2 + a$
5. $2x^2 + 21x$
6. $6x - 14y$
7. $2x^2 - x$
8. $2x^2 + 4x - 6$
9. $6x^2 - 7x + 2$
10. $5x^2 - 11x - 12$
11. $a^2 - ab - 6b^2$
12. $y^2 - 4$
13. $16x^2 + 40x + 25$
14. $5(x - 5)$
15. $2ab(a - 3b)$
16. $a(3b - 2c)$
17. $2a(2bc - 4b + 1)$
18. $(5 + y)(2x + 3)$
19. $(2 + 3y)(x + 3)$
20. $(4 + 3y)(2x + 3)$
21. $(4 + 3a)(b + 5)$
22. $(7a + 3)(2 + b)$
23. $(3a + 2)(2 + 3b)$
24. $(3 + 2y)(x - 5)$

25. $(3 + 2y)(x - 4)$
26. $(2 - 3y)(3x + 4)$
27. $(2 - a)(3b + 4)$
28. $(x - y)(x + y)$
29. $(p - q)(p + q)$
30. $(v - w)(v + w)$
31. $(x - 2y)(x + 2y)$
32. $(3a - b)(3a + b)$
33. $(r - 4s)(r + 4s)$
34. $2(a - 2b)(a + 2b)$
35. $4(2m - 3n)(2m + 3n)$
36. $5(x - 2y)(x + 2y)$
37. $(x^3 - y)(x^3 + y)$
38. 8
39. 5
40. 9
41. 8
42. $8a^2b^3c^3$
43. $\frac{7b^2}{a}$
44. $64a^6$
45. $\frac{6b}{a}$

Exam questions (page 21)

1 $3pq(4p - 5q)$
2 (a) $2x + 14$ (b) $9 - 6x + x^2$
3 (a) $4s^2 - 2s - 5$ (c) $8pq^3$
   (b) $2e^2 + 5ef - 3f^2$
4 $3x + 2(x + 45) = 415$ Small radiator = \$65
5 (a) $6a$ (b) $2a(2a - 1)$
6 $a - b$
7 (a) $12a^3b^4$ (b) $\dfrac{7a^2}{b}$
8 (a) $3x^2 + 10x - 8$ (b) $2y^2 - 7y + 3$
9 (a) $(5a - 3)(3 - 2b)$ (b) $(a - 2)(3 - 5b)$
10 (a) $2(5a - 3b)(5a + 3b)$ (b) $(x - y)(x + y)(x^2 + y^2)$
11 (a) $\frac{1}{2}$ (b) $\dfrac{p^3}{q}$
12 (a) $ab(b - 3a)$ (b) 1

Linear equations

Practice questions (pages 22–23)

1 $x = 5$ 7 $x = 8$ 13 $x = {}^-18$ 19 $x = 1$
2 $p = 2$ 8 $x = {}^-3$ 14 $m = 23$ 20 $x = 8$
3 $m = 2\frac{1}{4}$ 9 $x = 3$ 15 $p = 42$ 21 $x = 5$
4 $y = 8$ 10 $x = 2\frac{2}{5}$ 16 $x = 11$ 22 $x = \frac{24}{5} = 4\frac{4}{5}$
5 $m = 9$ 11 $x = \frac{1}{5}$ 17 $x = 16$
6 $p = 2$ 12 $x = {}^-4$ 18 $x = 8$

Exam questions (page 23)

1 $x = \frac{1}{2}$ 4 $y = 2$ 7 (a) $4x + 4 = 36$
2 $p = 6$ 5 $x = 3.5$ (b) $x = 8\,\text{cm}$
3 $m = 12$ 6 $x = 1$ (c) Area = $80\,\text{cm}^2$

Formulae

Practice questions (pages 24–25)

1 3
2 (a) 7·125
   (b) $-1\frac{7}{8}$ or -1.875
3 25
4 Let F = temperature in °F
   Let C = temperature in °C
   $C = \frac{5}{9}(F - 32)$
5 If $U_n = n$th term
   (a) $U_n = n^2$
   (b) $U_n = 3n^2$
   (c) $U_n = 3n - 1$
   (d) $U_n = 29 - 4n$
6 (a) $U_n = 2^n$
   (b) $U_n = 5 \times 2^{n-1}$
   (c) $U_n = n^2 + 1$
7 $c = y - mx$
8 $m = \dfrac{y - c}{x}$
9 $b = \dfrac{x + cd}{a}$
10 $c = \dfrac{ab - x}{d}$
11 $w = \dfrac{P - 2\ell}{2}$ or $\dfrac{P}{2} - \ell$
12 $h = \dfrac{3V}{\ell w}$
13 $r = \sqrt{\dfrac{A}{4\pi}}$
14 $r = \sqrt[3]{\dfrac{3V}{4\pi}}$
15 $x = \sqrt{y - a}$
16 $y = \dfrac{ax}{1 - b}$
17 $y = \dfrac{ax}{1 - a}$
18 $c = \dfrac{ab + bd}{a - d}$

Exam questions (page 25)

1 $n = \dfrac{P - 120}{4}$
2 144
3 $T = 20 + 30W$
4 $r = \sqrt{\dfrac{3V}{\pi h}}$
5 $U_n = 3n - 2$
6 (a) 1432·2
   (b) $y = \sqrt{\dfrac{x + 3}{4}}$
7 (a) $d = \dfrac{e - 3}{5}$
   (b) $d = \dfrac{4e + 7}{3 - 5e}$
8 (a) -32.3
   (b) $v = \dfrac{fu}{u - f}$
9 $n = 2 \times 3^t$

Direct and inverse proportion

Practice questions (pages 26–27)

1 192   5 240·1 m   8 0·5 m
2 90   6 1   9 0·2 lumens
3 43·75 litres   7 (a) 6   10 \$3562·50
4 1222 cm^2 (b) 16

Exam questions (page 27)

1 300   2 2000   3 72 m   4 (a) 400 N   (b) 424 m/s

Simultaneous equations and linear inequalities

Practice questions (pages 28–29)

1 (a) $x = 3, y = 2$ (c) $x = 2, y = {}^-1$ (e) $x = 2\frac{1}{2}, y = {}^-3\frac{1}{2}$
   (b) $x = 6, y = {}^-5$ (d) $x = 1, y = {}^-2$ (f) $x = 4, y = {}^-3$
2 (a) $x < 2$ (b) $x < \dfrac{{}^-3}{5}$ (c) $x \geqslant \frac{1}{6}$
3 $x > 1$ so smallest value is 2
4 $x \geqslant 5$ and $x \leqslant {}^-5$
5 ${}^-6 < x < {}^-2$

Exam questions (page 29)

1 $x = 3, y = \dfrac{{}^-1}{2}$
2 $x = {}^-1, y = 3$
3 (a) By substituting $x = 3$ and $y = 2$
   (b) $9p + 11q = 5$
   (c) $p = 3$ $q = -2$
4 $x > 2.5$
5 $x < 5.5$
6 $x < 6$ and $x > {}^-6$ or ${}^-6 < x < 6$

Quadratic equations

Practice questions (pages 30–31)

1 $(x + 5)(x + 1)$ 7 $3(x + 3)(x - 3)$ 13 ${}^-0.5$ or 7
2 $(x - 4)(x - 2)$ 8 3 or 6   14 2 or $\dfrac{{}^-5}{3}$
3 $(x - 5)(x + 3)$ 9 ${}^-4$ or 1   15 $\frac{1}{3}$ or $2\frac{1}{2}$
4 $(x + 3)(x - 3)$ 10 ${}^-4$ or ${}^-1$ 16 0 or ${}^-4$
5 $(3x - 2)(x - 1)$ 11 3 or 4   17 5 or ${}^-5$
6 $(x + 9)(x - 9)$ 12 2 or ${}^-5$

Questions 18 to 33 to 2 d.p.

18 5·16 or ${}^-1·16$ 24 0·16 or ${}^-4·16$ 30 1·39 or 0·36
19 ${}^-0·26$ or ${}^-7·74$ 25 ${}^-0·14$ or ${}^-5·86$ 31 5·18 or ${}^-0·68$
20 9·24 or 0·76   26 4·30 or 0·70   32 ${}^-0·17$ or ${}^-3·83$
21 2·62 or 0·38   27 ${}^-0·13$ or ${}^-3·87$ 33 ${}^-0·21$ or ${}^-3·79$
22 1·87 or 0·13   28 5·24 or 0·76
23 3·12 or ${}^-1·12$ 29 1·85 or ${}^-0·18$

34
There are no real solutions since you cannot find the square root of a negative number.

The graph does not cross the line $y = 0$.

Exam questions (page 31)

1 (a) $x = 2$ or 4
 (b) $x = 1\frac{1}{2}$ or $^-3$
2 (a) $5(x + 2)(x - 2)$
 (b) (i) $(x - 8)(x - 1)$ (ii) $x = 8$ or 1
3 (a) $6x^2 + 9x - 42$
 (b) (i) $x(x + 6)$ (ii) $x = 0$ or $^-6$
4 $x = 17 \cdot 73$ or $1 \cdot 27$ to 2 d.p.
5 (a) $3(x - 2)^2 - 10$
 (b) $x = 3 \cdot 83$ or $0 \cdot 17$ to 2 d.p.
6 (a) $y(15 - y) = 55$
  $15y - y^2 = 55$
  $y^2 - 15y + 55 = 0$
 (b) Length = $8 \cdot 62$ and width = $6 \cdot 38$ cm.
7 (a) Length (in m) = $22 - 2x$
  Area (in m²) = $x(22 - 2x) = 60$
  $22x - 2x^2 = 60$, $11x - x^2 = 30$, $x^2 - 11x + 30 = 0$
 (b) $x = 6$ or 5
 (c) The pen is 6 m by 10 m or 5 m by 12 m.

Algebraic fractions

Practice questions (page 32)

1 $\dfrac{x - 2}{x + 1}$ 3 $\dfrac{3x - 1}{x(x - 1)}$ 5 $x = {}^-0 \cdot 27$ or $3 \cdot 73$

2 $\dfrac{2(x + 2)}{2x + 1}$ 4 $\dfrac{3(2x - 1)}{(x + 1)(x - 2)}$ 6 $x = 1$ or $\frac{^-1}{2}$

Exam questions (page 32)

1 (b) $x = 2 \cdot 28$ or $^-3 \cdot 28$
2 $\dfrac{x}{x - 2}$
3 (a) $\dfrac{x + 3}{x + 2}$
 (b) $x = \frac{2}{3}$ or $^-3$

Sequences

Practice questions (pages 33–34)

1 6, 9, 12, 15 5 $2n + 1$ 9 (a) $2 \times 4^{n-1}$
2 $5n - 3$ 6 $10n$ (b) 5^{n-1}
3 89, $6n - 1$ 7 $5n - 9$ (c) $(n + 2)(n + 4)$
4 $44 - 4n$ 8 $35 - 3n$

Exam questions (page 34)

1 248, $5n - 2$
2 $5n - 4$
3 (a) $7n - 5$
 (b) If $7n - 5 = 300$, $7n = 305$, $n = 305 \div 7$,
  $n = 43 \cdot 57$. n is not a whole number, so 300 is
  not in the sequence.
4 (a) n^2 (b) $3n^2 + 1$
5 (a) $2n + 1$ (b) $2n^2 + n + 1$
6 (a) n^3 (b) $2n^3$ (c) $2n^3 - 3n$

Graphs of linear functions

Practice questions (pages 35–36)

1 (a) Gradient = $^-1 \cdot 5$, y-intercept = 3
 (b) Gradient = 2, y-intercept = 2
2 (a) $y = {}^-1 \cdot 5x + 3$ (b) $y = 2x + 2$
3 (a) $m = 4$, $c = {}^-1$ (d) $m = {}^-1$, $c = 4$
 (b) $m = 2$, $c = 3$ (e) $m = 1 \cdot 5$, $c = 2$
 (c) $m = 1$, $c = 0$ (f) $m = \frac{1}{4}$, $c = {}^-2 \cdot 5$
4 (a) $y = 3x - 3$ (b) $y = {}^-2x + 5$
5 (a), (d) and (f) are parallel; (c) and (e) are parallel

Exam questions (page 36)

1 (a) $^-2 \cdot 5$ (b) $y = {}^-2 \cdot 5x + 5$
2 (a) $m = {}^-2$, y-intercept = 4 (b) $y = {}^-2x - 1$
3 $y = {}^-2x + 6$

Graphical solution of simultaneous equations and linear inequalities

Practice questions (pages 37–38)

1 (a) 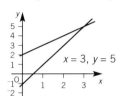 (b)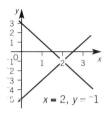

2 (a) 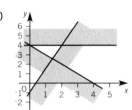 (b)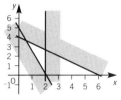

Exam questions (page 38)

1 (a)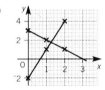

$x = 1\frac{1}{4}$, $y = 1\frac{3}{4}$

 (b)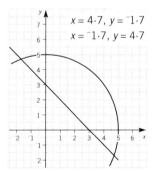

2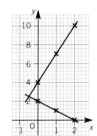

$x = {}^-0 \cdot 5$, $y = 2 \cdot 5$

3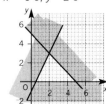

4 $x + y \leqslant 3$
 $y \geqslant x$
 $x \geqslant {}^-2$

Linear programming

Practice questions (pages 39–40)

1 $x \geqslant 5$, $y \geqslant 5$, $x + y < 15$

2 $x + y \leqslant 6$, $24x + 53y \geqslant 190$

3 $y > x$, $x + y \leqslant 600$, $5x + 8y \geqslant 3200$

4

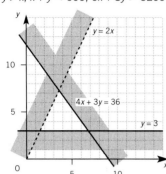

5

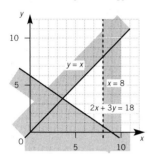

6

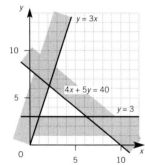

7 (a) The points (4, 6), (3, 5), (4, 5), (5, 5), (3, 4), (4, 4), (5, 4), (6, 4), (2, 3), (3, 3), (4, 3), (5, 3) and (6, 3) marked.

   (b) (i) (4, 6)   **(ii)** 16

8 (a) (6, 2)   **(b)** 18

9 (3, 3), (4, 4)

Exam questions (page 41)

1 (a) $x + 2y \leqslant 28$, $3x + y \leqslant 24$

   (b)

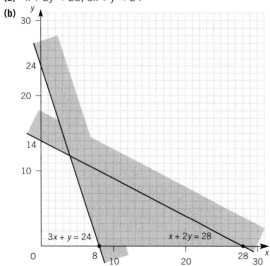

   (c) (i) $200   **(ii)** 4 type A and 12 type B

Answers

2 (a) (i) $1000 is available so $10x + 25y \leqslant 1000$. Dividing by 5 gives $2x + 5y \leqslant 200$.

     (ii) $y \geqslant x$ and $x + y \geqslant 50$

   (b)

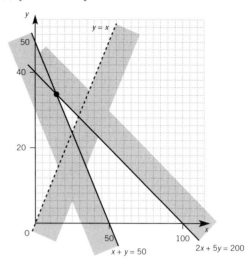

   (c) 33

3 (a) (i) x small vehicles will carry $5x$ people and y large vehicles will carry $8y$ people. 60 people must fit into these vehicles so $5x + 8y \geqslant 60$.

     (ii) $600x + 300y \geqslant 4500$ or $2x + y \geqslant 15$, $x \leqslant 8$, $y \leqslant 7$

   (b)

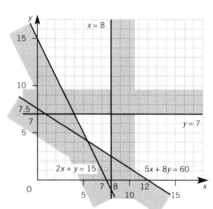

   (c) (i) The points (4, 7), (5, 7), (6, 7), (7, 7), (8, 7), (5, 6), (6, 6), (7, 6), (8, 6), (5, 5), (6, 5), (7, 5), (8, 5), (6, 4), (7, 4), (8, 4) and (8, 3) marked.

     (ii) 10

     (iii) 5 of each type or 6 small and 4 large vehicles.

4 (a) $x > y$, $x + 3y \geqslant 30$

   (b)

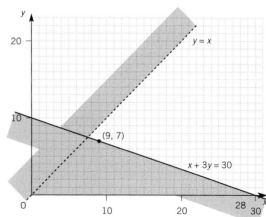

   (c) (i) 23 hrs

     (ii) 9 individual photos and 7 sets

Answers

Interpreting graphs

Practice questions (pages 42–43)

1 **(a)** Accelerated at 0·8 m/s² for 25 seconds to 20 m/s.
   Constant speed of 20 m/s for 15 seconds.
   Retarded at 2 m/s² for 10 seconds to stop.

(b) Single tap filling at 4 litres/minute for 5 minutes
   followed by both taps filling at 8 litres/minutes for
   $2\frac{1}{2}$ minutes. Constant at 40 litres for $12\frac{1}{2}$ minutes.
   Emptied at 8 litres/minute in 5 minutes.

2
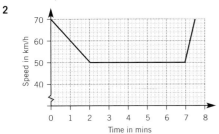

3 550 m

4
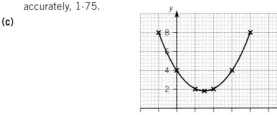

Exam questions (page 43)

1 **(a)**
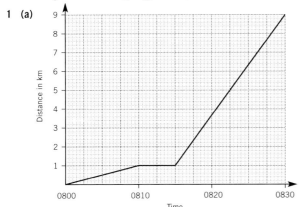

(b) $3\frac{2}{3}$ km or 3·7 km.

2 e.g. A car accelerates and then travels at a steady speed and
   then stops suddenly (crashes, etc.).

3 **(a)**   **(b)**   **(c)**
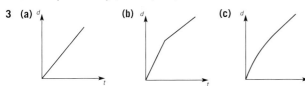

Quadratic and other functions

Practice questions (pages 44–46)

1 **(a)** *y*-values: 8, 4, 2, 2, 4, 8

(b) So that the minimum point on the graph can be plotted
   accurately, 1·75.

(c)

2 *y*-values: 18, 7, 0, ⁻3, ⁻2, 3, 12, 25
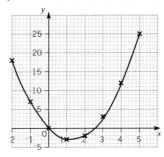

3 **(a)** $x = 0$ or 3
   (b) $x = {}^-0\cdot8$ or 3·8 to 1 d.p.
   (c) $x = 0\cdot6$ or 3·4

4 **(a)** $x = 0$ or 2·5
   (b) $x = 2\cdot3$ or 0·2 to 1 d.p.
   (c) $x = {}^-0\cdot1$ or 3·6

5
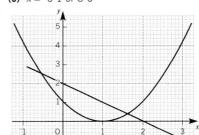

$x = {}^-0\cdot6$ or 1·6

6
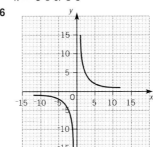

7
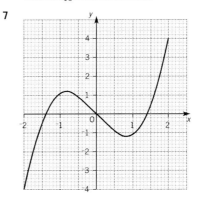

Roots $x = 0$ or ± 1·4 to 1 d.p; positive
root 1·41 to 2 d.p.

8
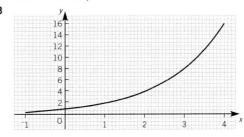

$x = 3\cdot3$

9

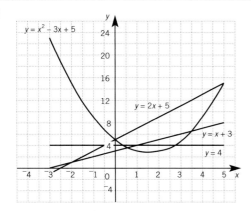

(a) $x = 0.3$ or 2.6 (b) $x = 0.6$ or 3.4 (c) $x = 0$ or 5

10

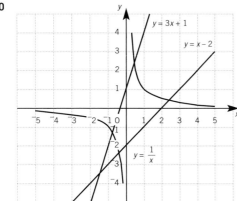

(a) $x = {}^-0.7$ or 0.4 (b) $x = 2.4$ or ${}^-0.4$

11

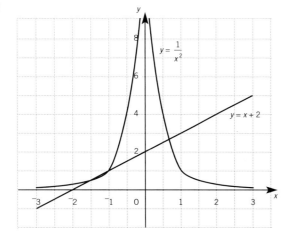

$x = {}^-1.5, {}^-1$ or 0.6

1 (a) ${}^-5$ 0 [3] 4 3 [0] ${}^-5$

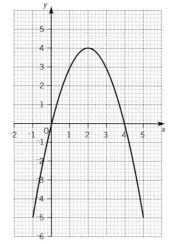

    (b) (i) 2   **(ii)** 0.6 and 3.4

2 (a) T   **(b)** Q   **(c)** U

3 (a)

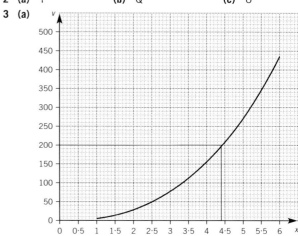

    (b) 4.4 cm, 4.4 cm, 10.4 cm

4 (a)

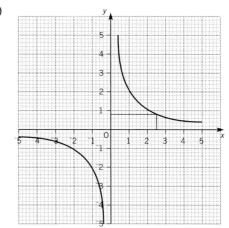

    (b) 2.5

5 (a) $({}^-2, {}^-1)$ in table

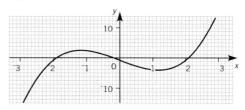

    (b) ${}^-2$ to ${}^-1.7$, ${}^-0.4$ to ${}^-0.2$, 2.0 to 2.2

    (c) $y = 2x + 2$ drawn, ${}^-2.3$ to ${}^-2.0$, ${}^-0.6$ to ${}^-0.3$, 2.5 to 2.8

6

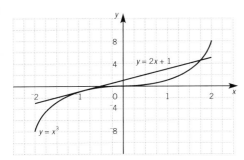

$x = {}^-1, {}^-0.6$ or 1.6

7

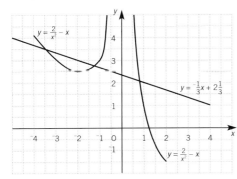

$x = {}^-3.2, {}^-1.1$ or 0.8

Graphs – gradient and area

Practice questions (pages 48–50)

Answers read from graphs may not be exactly as given here but should approximate to these.

1 (a) 3   (b) 12

2 (a) $^-3$ (b) $^-0.75$ (c) $^-0.75$

3 (a) $^-5$ (b) 1

4 (a) 10   (b) 2   (c) 10

5 (a) $23\,\text{ms}^{-1}$ (b) $70\,\text{ms}^{-1}$

6 (a) $4\,\text{ms}^{-2}$ (b) $1.1\,\text{ms}^{-2}$

7 20

8 27

9 10

10 35 m

Exam questions (pages 51–52)

1 (a) $^-1.6\,\text{ms}^{-2}$ (b) 19 m

2 (a)

Time (*t* hours)	0	1	2	3	4	5
Number of bacteria (*n*)	20	60	180	540	1620	4860

   (b) $n = 20 \times 3^t$

(c)

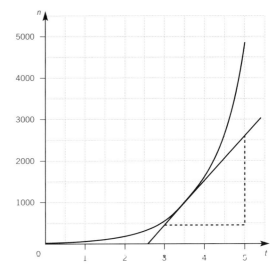

(d) (i) 1075

     (ii) The rate of increase in bacteria per hour.

3 (a) $p = 29$, $q = 24$, $r = 50$

   (b)

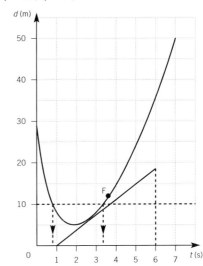

(c) F on graph, 3.6 seconds

(d) 2.55 seconds

(e) 3.7 m/s

4 (a) $1.08\,\text{m/s}^2$

   (b) Approximately 1680 m

5 (a) Approximately 20 km

   (b) Approximately 9.45 a.m.

Functions

Practice questions (pages 53–55)

1 (a) 36   (b) $^-14$ (c) 1

2 (a) $^-21$ (b) $^-3$ (c) $3 - 8x$

3 (a) 9   (b) $3(6x - 7)$ (c) $3(2x - 9)$

4 (a) 2   (b) 0.4   (c) 4

5 (a) 73   (c) $12x^2 - 2$ (e) $12x^2 + 3$

   (b) 1   (d) $3x^2 + 18x + 25$

6 (a) 2   (c) $^-3$

   (b) $^-2$ (d) 16

7 (a) 1   (b) $^-5$ (c) (i) $x - 2$

                                     (ii) $x - 2$

8 (a) 50   (b) $^-18$ (c) (i) $10x + 10$

                                     (ii) $10x - 13$

9 (a) 23   (b) 6   (c) (i) $2x + 13$

                                     (ii) $2x + 5$

10 (a) $^-23$ **(b)** 22 **(c)(i)** $^-23 - 6x$
(ii) $10 - 6x$

11 (a) $4x^2 - 3$ **(b)** $16x^2 - 24x + 9$
12 (a) $2x^2 - 4x + 3$ **(b)** $4x^2$
13 (a) $\frac{x-2}{7}$ **(b)** 0 **(c)** $\frac{^-2}{7}$
14 (a) $4(x+1)$ **(b)** 9 **(c)** $^-16$
15 (a) $\frac{x}{3} - 2$ **(c)** $\frac{x}{12} + 2$

(b) $\frac{4x+5}{2}$ **(d)** $\sqrt{\frac{x-3}{5}}$

Exam questions (page 55)

1 (a) $\frac{x+1}{2}$ **(b)** $4x^2 - 4x$
2 (a)(i) 27 **(ii)** 3 **(b)(i)** $2x^{\frac{2}{3}} - 5$ **(ii)** x^3
3 (a) $^-8$ **(c)** $3x - 2$
 (b) $\frac{x+5}{3}$ **(d)** $x = 5$
4 (a) $^-1$ **(b)** $\frac{3x-5}{2}$
5 (a) $\frac{x-1}{3}$ **(c)** $18x^2 + 12x + 2$
 (b) 25 **(d)** $9x + 4$
6 (a) $^-1$ **(c)** $3x + 15$ **(e)** $\frac{2x}{3} - 9$
 (b) $\frac{x-1}{2}$ **(d)** $^-9$

Sets and Venn diagrams

Practice questions (pages 56–58)

1 {10, 12, 14, 16, 18, 20}
2 When $x = 4$, $y = 2 \times 4 - 7 = 1$, so $(4, 1) \in \{(x, y): y = 2x - 7\}$.
3

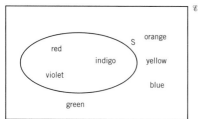

4 (a) {1, 4, 5, 7, 8, 9, 10}
 (b)(i) $\in$ **(ii)** $\notin$ **(iii)** $\in$
5 (a) {3}
 (b) { }, or $\varnothing$
 (c) {1, 2, 3, 5, 6}
 (d) {4, 6, 7}
6 { }, {a}, {b}, {c}, {a, b}, {a, c}, {b, c}, {a, b, c}
7

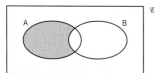

Exam questions (page 58)

1

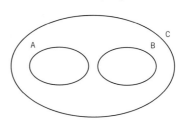

2 (a) {6, 12}
 (b) {1, 5, 7, 11}
3

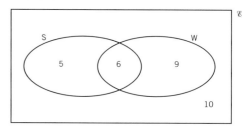

Total = 5 + 6 + 9 + 10 = 30

4 (a)

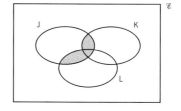

 (b) S' ∪ T
 (c)

5 students study chemistry but not French.

Matrices

Practice questions (pages 59–61)

1 (a) 2×4 **(b)** 4×2 **(c)** 3×4
2 $\begin{pmatrix} 5 & 8 & 10 \\ 11 & 6 & 9 \end{pmatrix}$
3 $\begin{pmatrix} 86 & 58 & 102 \\ 92 & 59 & 98 \\ 95 & 56 & 116 \end{pmatrix}$
4 $\begin{pmatrix} 3 & 8 & 2 \\ 2 & 10 & 1 \\ 4 & 11 & 2 \\ 2 & 9 & 3 \end{pmatrix}$
5 (a) $\begin{pmatrix} 11 & 6 & 7 & 6 \\ 7 & 10 & 10 & 7 \end{pmatrix}$ **(c)** $\begin{pmatrix} 11 & 4 & 12 & 3 \\ 12 & 5 & 7 & 3 \\ 6 & 8 & ^-1 & 8 \end{pmatrix}$
 (b) $\begin{pmatrix} 37 & 12 \\ 6 & 35 \\ 25 & 36 \end{pmatrix}$ **(d)** $\begin{pmatrix} 13 & 12 \\ ^-2 & 10 \end{pmatrix}$
6 (a) $\begin{pmatrix} 2 & ^-2 \\ ^-1 & ^-2 \end{pmatrix}$ **(c)** $\begin{pmatrix} 7 & 7 \\ 19 & ^-25 \\ 2 & ^-3 \end{pmatrix}$
 (b) $\begin{pmatrix} ^-7 & 2 & 0 \\ ^-1 & 7 & ^-8 \\ ^-1 & 5 & ^-3 \\ 1 & ^-7 & 2 \end{pmatrix}$ **(d)** $\begin{pmatrix} 13 & 0 & 11 & ^-6 \\ 3 & 0 & ^-5 & ^-8 \end{pmatrix}$

Answers

7 (a) $\begin{pmatrix} 13 & 19 \\ 25 & 37 \end{pmatrix}$ (d) $\begin{pmatrix} 24 \\ 26 \end{pmatrix}$ (g) $\begin{pmatrix} 9 & 12 & 6 \\ 1 & ^-24 & 14 \end{pmatrix}$

(b) $\begin{pmatrix} 21 & ^-2 \\ ^-7 & 18 \end{pmatrix}$ (e) $(^-11 \ \ ^-6)$ (h) $\begin{pmatrix} 10 & ^-7 & 16 \\ ^-5 & 28 & ^-15 \\ 10 & 24 & 32 \end{pmatrix}$

(c) Not possible   (f) $(8 \ \ 5)$

8 (a) 7   (e) 26
(b) 4   (f) –7
(c) ‾1   (g) 23
(d) 3   (h) ‾2

9 (a) $\begin{pmatrix} 3 & ^-5 \\ ^-4 & 7 \end{pmatrix}$ (d) $\begin{pmatrix} ^-2 & ^-3 \\ ^-5 & ^-8 \end{pmatrix}$ (g) $\begin{pmatrix} 3 & ^-3.5 \\ ^-2 & ^-2.5 \end{pmatrix}$

(b) $\begin{pmatrix} 5 & ^-3 \\ ^-3 & 2 \end{pmatrix}$ (e) $\begin{pmatrix} 1.25 & ^-0.5 \\ ^-2 & 1 \end{pmatrix}$ (h) $\begin{pmatrix} 2.5 & 4 \\ 2 & ^-3 \end{pmatrix}$

(c) $\begin{pmatrix} 4 & ^-9 \\ ^-3 & 7 \end{pmatrix}$ (f) $\begin{pmatrix} 0.5 & ^-0.4 \\ ^-0.5 & 0.6 \end{pmatrix}$

Exam questions (page 61)

1 (a) $\mathbf{AB} = \begin{pmatrix} 19 \\ 14 \end{pmatrix}$ (b) $\mathbf{A}^{-1} = \begin{pmatrix} ^-1 & ^-1 \\ ^-\frac{1}{2} & \frac{3}{4} \end{pmatrix}$

2 (a) $\mathbf{M} = \begin{pmatrix} ^-3 & 2 \\ ^-1 & ^-2 \end{pmatrix}$ (b) $\mathbf{N} = \begin{pmatrix} \frac{1}{4} & \frac{1}{4} \\ ^-\frac{1}{8} & \frac{3}{8} \end{pmatrix}$

3 (a) $x = ^-4$ (c) $\mathbf{Q}^{-1} = \begin{pmatrix} \frac{3}{5} & \frac{2}{5} \\ \frac{2}{5} & \frac{3}{5} \end{pmatrix}$

(b) |**R**|, the determinant of **R**, is zero.

4 (a) $p = ^-3, q = ^-17$ (b) $\mathbf{X}^{-1} = \begin{pmatrix} ^-\frac{1}{5} & ^-\frac{2}{5} \\ \frac{4}{5} & \frac{3}{5} \end{pmatrix}$

5 (a) The number of columns in **A** is not the same as the number of rows in **B**.

(b) (i) $\mathbf{B}^2 = \begin{pmatrix} 17 & ^-32 \\ ^-16 & 33 \end{pmatrix}$ (ii) $\mathbf{B}^{-1} = \begin{pmatrix} \frac{5}{7} & \frac{4}{7} \\ \frac{2}{7} & \frac{3}{7} \end{pmatrix}$

Properties of triangles and other shapes

Practice questions (pages 62–63)

There are other correct reasons for the answers in questions 1 to 4.
1 $a = 104°$ (exterior angle = sum of opposite interior angles)
$b = 52°$ (isosceles triangle and exterior angle = sum of opposite interior angles)
2 $c = 37°$ (alternate angles are equal)
$d = 110°$ (exterior angle = sum of opposite interior angles)
3 $e = 17°$ (corresponding angles are equal)
$f = 49°$ (alternate angles are equal)
4 $p + q = x$ (exterior angle = sum of opposite interior angles)
$p = q$ (base angles of isosceles triangle are equal)
So $p = \frac{1}{2}x°$
$g = 180 - \frac{1}{2}x°$ (angles on a straight line = 180°)
5 135°
6 104°
7 15 sides
8 102°
9 $\frac{8}{4} = \frac{20}{10} = 2$
Sides in corresponding positions to the right angle are in proportion.
10 $MN = 5 \times \frac{9}{6} = 7.5$ $PQ = 4 \times \frac{6}{9} = \frac{8}{3}$ (= 2.7)

Exam questions (page 64)

1 (a) 72°   (b) Isosceles
2 $x = 53°$ (corresponding angles are equal)
$y = 96°$ (exterior angle = sum of opposite interior angles)
3 $n = 30$
4 $x = 116°, y = 128°$
5 $x = 69°$ (exterior angle = sum of interior angles)
$y = 13.5°$ (isosceles triangle and exterior angle = sum of interior angles)
6 In triangle ABC and triangle ECD
BC = CD (given)
angle ABC = EDC (alternate angles)
angle ACB = angle DCE (vertically oposite)
So triangle ABC is congruent to triangle EDC.
7 (a) Angle ADE = angle ABC (corresponding angles, DE parallel to BC)
Angle AED = angle ACB (corresponding angles, DE parallel to BC)
Angle A is common
Triangles are similar as corresponding angles are equal.

(b) $\frac{AD}{AB} = \frac{1}{4}$, BC = 4 × DE = 12 cm.

Pythagoras and trigonometry

Practice questions (pages 65–66)

1 (a) 3·87 cm   (b) 29·0°
2 (a) 3·06 cm   (b) 6·73 cm
3 (a) 3·77 cm   (b) 46·7°
4 (a) 8·54 m   (b) 1·07 m
5 64·6°
6 (a) 2·57 m   (b) 66°
7 (a) 22·46 m   (b) 30·4°
8 6·85 cm
9 331 m

Exam questions (page 67)

1 (a) 17·7 m   (b) 8·94 m
2 (a) 5·2 m   (b) 3·1 m²
3 (a) 21·2 km   (b) 155 km²

Properties of circles

Practice questions (pages 68–69)

1 17 cm
2 4·90 cm
3 50°
4 8·94 cm
5 20°
6 (a) 29°   (b) 119°
7 angle CDA = 65° (opposite angles of a cyclic quadrilateral)
angle CDE = 180 – 65 = 115° (angles on a straight line)
8 angle ADX = angle BCX (angles in the same segment)
angle DAX = angle CBX (angles in the same segment)
angle DXA = angle CXB (vertically opposite angles)
(or any of these replaced by 'angle sum of triangle')
Therefore triangles are similar (all angles are equal)
9 $a = 65°, b = 25°, c = 130°$

Exam questions (page 70)

1 $x = 36°$ (angles in the same segment)
$y = 72°$ (angle at centre = twice angle at circumference)
$z = 62°$ (radius at right angles to tangent)
2 (a) 56°   (b) 124°   (c) 22°

3 $a = 27°$, $b = 63°$, $c = 54°$, $d = 36°$

4 (a) $x°$ (b) $90° - x°$ (c) $x°$ (d) $2x°$

5 (a) $90°$ (angle in a semi-circle)
     (b) $180° - 2x°$

3D shapes

Practice questions (pages 71–72)

1 5 cm   **5** 11·9 cm
2 265 cm³   **6** 184 cm³
3 2 cm   **7** (a) 4·8 cm   (b) 10 000 cm² = 1 m²
4 452·4 cm³   **8** 240 cm²

Exam questions (page 73)

1 0·88 m³   **5** (a) 32 cm   (b) 62 500 cm³
2 96 cm²   **6** (a) 2 cm   (b) 147 cm³
3 230·9 cm³
4 28·2 cm³

Transformations and coordinates

Practice questions (pages 74–80)

1
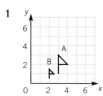

2 (a) Reflection in y-axis.
     (b) Reflection in $x = ^-2$.
     (c) Enlargement with centre (0, 3), scale factor 3.
     (d) Enlargement with centre (0, 3), scale factor $\frac{1}{3}$.
     (e) Translation by $\begin{pmatrix} ^-5 \\ 2 \end{pmatrix}$.
     (f) Translation by $\begin{pmatrix} 2 \\ ^-6 \end{pmatrix}$.
     (g) Translation by $\begin{pmatrix} 4 \\ 0 \end{pmatrix}$.
     (h) Rotation through 90° clockwise about (1·5, ⁻1·5).
     (i) Translation by $\begin{pmatrix} ^-4 \\ 0 \end{pmatrix}$.
     (j) Reflection in $y = x$.
     (k) Enlargement with centre (⁻1, 6), scale factor 3.

3 (a) Stretch factor = 3
     (b) Stretch factor = 1·5

4 (a) Stretch factor = 2, fixed line $y = 2$
     (b) Stretch factor = 1·5, fixed line $y = 1$

5 (a) Shear factor = 2 to the right
     (b) Shear factor = 3 to the right

6 Translation of $\begin{pmatrix} 3 \\ 1 \end{pmatrix}$.

7 Rotation through 180° about (3, 2).

8 Reflection in $y = x$.

9 Reflection in $y = ^-x$.

10
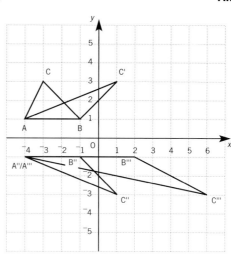

11
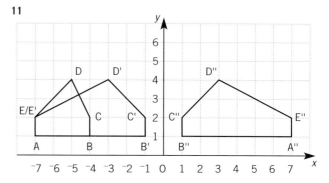

12 (a) A'(2, 0), B'(4, 0), C'(4, ⁻2), D'(2, ⁻2)
      (b) A"(0, ⁻2), B"(0, ⁻4), C"(2, ⁻4), D"(2, ⁻2)
      (c) A'''(0, ⁻2), B'''(0, ⁻4), C'''(⁻2, ⁻4), D'''(⁻2, ⁻2)
      (d) $R = \begin{pmatrix} 0 & ^-1 \\ ^-1 & 0 \end{pmatrix}$, $S = \begin{pmatrix} 0 & 1 \\ 1 & 0 \end{pmatrix}$
      (e) (0, ⁻2), (0, ⁻4), (⁻2, ⁻4) (⁻2, ⁻2), reflection in the line $y = ^-x$
      (f) (0, 2), (0, 4), (2, 4), (2, 2), reflection in the line $y = x$

13 (a) (i) (⁻2, ⁻1), (⁻4, ⁻1), (⁻4, ⁻4)
          (ii) Rotation of 180° about the origin
      (b) (i) (2, ⁻1), (4, ⁻1), (4, ⁻4)
          (ii) Reflection in the x-axis

14 (a) (i) (4·5, 4)   (ii) 8·06 to 2 d.p.
      (b) (i) (3·5, ⁻2)   (ii) 12·04 to 2 d.p.
      (c) (i) (1, ⁻1)   (ii) 10

15 (a) Area   (b) Neither   (c) Volume

16 9 cm²

17 125 ml

18 (a) 1·6 m²   (b) 50 cm³

Exam questions (pages 80–81)

1 (a) (⁻0·5, 2)
     (b) $BC^2 = 3^2 + 5^2 = 34$
          $BC = \sqrt{34} = 5·83$ units to 2 d.p.

2 (a) Enlargement centre (0, 0), scale factor 0·5.
     (b) Rotation through 180° about (4, 1).

3 (a) and (d)

4 19·0 cm

5 (a) 20·3 cm²   (b) 911 g

6 (a) $\begin{pmatrix} ^-1 & 0 \\ 1 & 1 \end{pmatrix}$ (b) $\begin{pmatrix} 0 & 1 \\ ^-1 & 0 \end{pmatrix}$
     (c) Reflection in the line $y = x$
     (d) **QP** gives a reflection in the line $y = x$.
          PQ gives a reflection in the line $y = ^-x$.
          The inverse of a reflection in the line $y = x$ is itself a
          reflection in the line $y = x$, not reflection in the line $y = ^-x$.

Answers

7 (a) Reflection in the line $x + y = 0$, i.e. $y = {}^-x$

(b) $\begin{pmatrix} 0 & 1 \\ {}^-1 & 0 \end{pmatrix}$

(c) **(i)** Scale factor is ${}^-2$

(ii) Centre is (1, 5)

(d) **(i)** Coordinates are (8, 6), (10, 6), (11, 15)

(ii) 9 sq units

(iii) $\begin{pmatrix} \frac{1}{2} & \frac{{}^-1}{6} \\ 0 & \frac{1}{3} \end{pmatrix}$

8 (a) **(i)** A shear along the x-axis direction, shear factor = ${}^-2$
(or a shear with the x-axis as the invariant line)

(ii) A shear along the y-axis direction, shear factor = 2
(or a shear with the y-axis as the invariant line)

(b) $\begin{pmatrix} 1 & {}^-2 \\ 0 & 2 \end{pmatrix}$

9 (a) **(i)** A parallelogram

(ii) A shear with the x-axis as the invariant line and shear factor 1

(b) **(i)** The original rectangle

(ii) A shear with the x-axis as the invariant line and shear factor ${}^-1$

Vectors

Practice questions (pages 82–83)

1 (a) $\begin{pmatrix} 1 \\ 7 \end{pmatrix}, \begin{pmatrix} 3 \\ 3 \end{pmatrix}$ **(b)** 2·24 units

2 $\overrightarrow{AB} = \begin{pmatrix} 6 \\ 9 \end{pmatrix} = 3\begin{pmatrix} 2 \\ 3 \end{pmatrix}$, so parallel

3 (a) $\mathbf{b} - \mathbf{a}$

(b) $\overrightarrow{AC} = 4\mathbf{b} - 4\mathbf{a} = 4\overrightarrow{AB}$, so A, B and C lie in a straight line.

4 (a) 5·4   **(b)** 5   **(c)** 8·5

5 (a) 7·6   **(b)** 7·8   **(c)** 3·6

6 (a) 2·2   **(c)** 9·4   **(e)** 27·0
    (b) 12·0   **(d)** 8·5

7

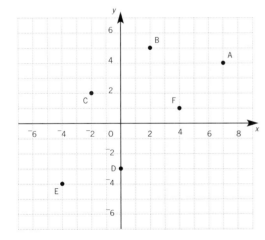

8 (a) $\overrightarrow{OA} = \begin{pmatrix} 7 \\ 4 \end{pmatrix}$, $\overrightarrow{OB} = \begin{pmatrix} 3 \\ 1 \end{pmatrix}$, $\overrightarrow{OC} = \begin{pmatrix} 5 \\ {}^-2 \end{pmatrix}$, $\overrightarrow{OD} = \begin{pmatrix} 4 \\ {}^-4 \end{pmatrix}$,

$\overrightarrow{OE} = \begin{pmatrix} {}^-1 \\ {}^-6 \end{pmatrix}$, $\overrightarrow{OF} = \begin{pmatrix} 2 \\ {}^-4 \end{pmatrix}$, $\overrightarrow{OG} = \begin{pmatrix} {}^-6 \\ {}^-3 \end{pmatrix}$, $\overrightarrow{OH} = \begin{pmatrix} {}^-4 \\ 0 \end{pmatrix}$,

$\overrightarrow{OI} = \begin{pmatrix} {}^-7 \\ 3 \end{pmatrix}$, $\overrightarrow{OJ} = \begin{pmatrix} 3 \\ 5 \end{pmatrix}$

(b) (i) $\begin{pmatrix} 11 \\ 4 \end{pmatrix}$ **(vi)** $\begin{pmatrix} 1 \\ {}^-9 \end{pmatrix}$

(ii) $\begin{pmatrix} 10 \\ {}^-2 \end{pmatrix}$ **(vii)** $\begin{pmatrix} {}^-9 \\ {}^-4 \end{pmatrix}$

(iii) $\begin{pmatrix} 11 \\ 1 \end{pmatrix}$ **(viii)** $\begin{pmatrix} {}^-9 \\ 2 \end{pmatrix}$

(iv) $\begin{pmatrix} 8 \\ {}^-4 \end{pmatrix}$ **(ix)** $\begin{pmatrix} {}^-11 \\ 7 \end{pmatrix}$

(v) $\begin{pmatrix} {}^-8 \\ {}^-10 \end{pmatrix}$ **(x)** $\begin{pmatrix} 3 \\ 8 \end{pmatrix}$

Exam questions (page 84)

1 (a) (4, 6) (1, 3·5) (0, ${}^-0.5$)   **(b)** $\begin{pmatrix} {}^-2 \\ {}^-8 \end{pmatrix}\begin{pmatrix} {}^-1 \\ {}^-4 \end{pmatrix}$

(c) MN is parallel to BC and BC = 2 × MN.

2 (a) (i) $2\mathbf{b}$ **(ii)** $\mathbf{a} - \mathbf{b}$ **(iii)** $\mathbf{b} + \frac{1}{2}\mathbf{a}$

(b) $\frac{1}{3}(\mathbf{a} + 2\mathbf{b})$ **(c)** Collinear, and OM = 1·5 × OH.

3 (a)

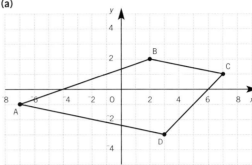

(b) (i) $\overrightarrow{AC,} = \begin{pmatrix} 14 \\ 2 \end{pmatrix}$ **(ii)** $\overrightarrow{DB,} = \begin{pmatrix} {}^-1 \\ 5 \end{pmatrix}$

(c) $|\overrightarrow{AC}| = 14.1$

4 (a)

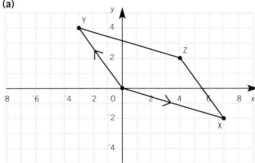

(b) $\overrightarrow{YX} = \begin{pmatrix} 10 \\ {}^-6 \end{pmatrix}$

(c) $\overrightarrow{OZ} = \begin{pmatrix} 4 \\ 2 \end{pmatrix}$

Measures

Practice questions (pages 85–86)

1 4000 mm^2 **10** 5·3125 (5·31) cm^3

2 15 000 cm^2 **11** 68·3 people/km^2

3 1500 litres   **12 (a)** 72·5 to 73·5 g

4 5·254 m^3 **(b)** 4·25 to 4·35 litres

5 5 cm^2 **(c)** 7·045 to 7·055 m

6 15 300 mm^3 **13** 25·65 to 25·75 s

7 6 300 000 cm^3 **14** Lower = 3·67

8 24 m^3 Upper = 4·62

9 299 cm   **15** 3·11 to 3·20 cm

Exam questions (page 86)

1 (a) 4 410 000 mm^3 **(b)** 0·00441 m^3

2 9 kg

3 5·10

4 Lower = 43·6 people/km^2 Upper = 46·1 people/km^2

5 3246 pools

Constructions

Practice questions (pages 87–88)

Answers should be within ± 1mm or ± 1°

1 5·4 cm; 85°; 45°   **4** 69°; 6·4 cm; 58°

2 40°; 4·7 cm; 8·8 cm   **5** 5·7 cm

3 117°; 36°; 27°   **6** 5·8 cm

Exam questions (page 88)

1 AX = 4·8 cm

2 MZ = 2·9 cm

2D shapes

Practice questions (pages 89–90)

1 42 cm²

2 0.77 m²

3 251·3 m²

4 114·6°

5 15·3 cm

Exam questions (page 90)

1 15·7 cm²

2 6398 km

3 445·8 m²

4 402 m²

5 202·4 m²

Loci

Practice questions (page 91)

1 Circle, centre P, radius 4 cm drawn.

2 Perpendicular bisector of AB drawn and the side of it including A shaded.

3 Bisector of the angle drawn.

4 Shore line drawn running SE to NW.
Locus of boat drawn – a line parallel to the shore and 500 m from it.

Exam questions (page 92)

1

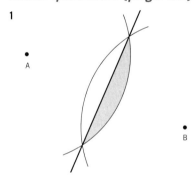

2

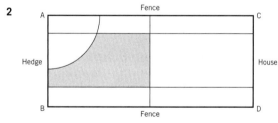

3

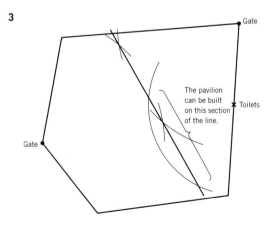

Processing and representing data

Practice questions (pages 93–95)

1 (a) 42, 66, 55, 15, 6, 1·6

(b)

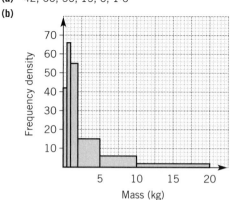

2 (a) 1·6, 4, 5, 2·5, 0·85

(b)

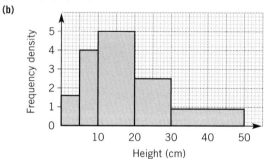

(c) 18·5 cm

3 (a)

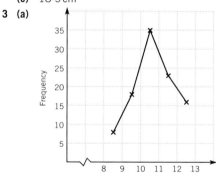

(b) 10·71 cm

4 (a)

(b) 186·2 cm

Answers

5 **(a)** Cumulative frequencies: 8, 23, 56, 78, 95, 100.

(b)

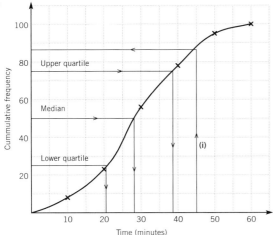

(c) **(i)** 13 or 14   **(ii)** 28   **(iii)** 38 − 21 = 17

6 **(a)** 84

(b) Median = 56, interquartile range = 70 − 41 = 29

Exam questions (pages 96–97)

1 **(a)** **(i)** [9], 22, 43, 60, 70, 78, 80

(ii)

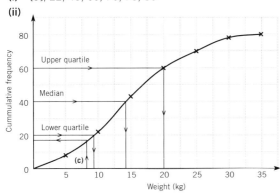

(b) **(i)** 14 to 14·8 kg

(ii) 10.5 to 11 is acceptable

(c) 63 to 65 is acceptable

2 72·5 kg

3 **(a)** **(i)** $4 < t \leqslant 5$ minutes

(ii)

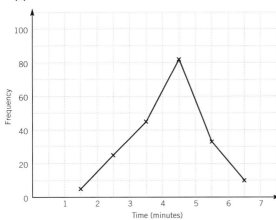

(b) 4·22 minutes

(c) **(i)** [0], [5], 30, 75, 157, 190, [200]

(ii)

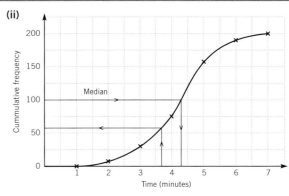

(d) **(i)** 4·2 to 4·5 minutes

(ii) 0·69 to 0·75

4 Frequency densities 2·8, 4·1, 5·9, 3·5, 0·53

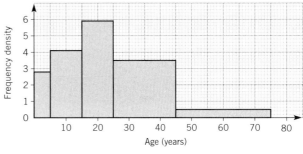

5 Frequency densities 12, 16, 9·5, 4, 1·5

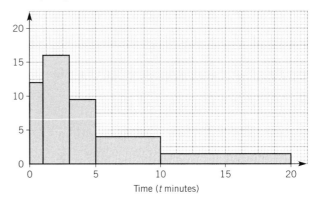

6 28, [60], 132, 108, 60

Probability

Practice questions (pages 98–100)

1 0·148

Yes, there should be roughly the same frequency for each number, but there are nearly twice as many 4s as 3s.

2 **(a)** 43   **(b)** 0·288, to 2.d.p. or more

3

Main Course	Dessert
SP	BC
SP	CG
SP	T
MC	BC
MC	CG
MC	T

4

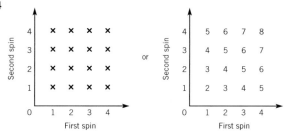

(a) $\frac{1}{16}$ (b) $\frac{3}{16}$

5 (a) **Machine A**   **Machine B**

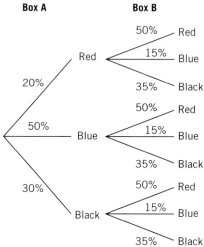

Machine A tree diagram:
0·97 — Fills with jam; 0·98 — Coats with sugar, 0·02 — Misses
0·03 — Misses; 0·98 — Coats with sugar, 0·02 — Misses

(b) 0·0006   (c) 0·0488

6 (a) $\frac{8}{125}$ (b) $\frac{27}{125}$ (c) $\frac{54}{125}$

7 (a) $\frac{1}{15}$ or equivalent   (b) $\frac{31}{45}$ or equivalent

8 (a) $\frac{4}{25}$ (b) $\frac{23}{50}$

9 $\frac{8}{15}$

10 $\frac{10}{21}$

Exam questions (page 101)

1 (a) 0·3 added to first set of branches, 0·8 and 0·2 to each of second sets.

(b) (i) 0·56   (ii) 0·38

2 (a) $\frac{6}{10}$ and $\frac{4}{10}$ on first set of branches, $\frac{2}{3}, \frac{1}{3}, \frac{1}{4}, \frac{3}{4}$ on second set with 'goes', 'not go' or other suitable labels.

(b) (i) $\frac{2}{5}$ or equivalent   (ii) $\frac{3}{10}$ or equivalent

3 (a) $\frac{1}{7}$ or equivalent

(b) $\frac{31}{105}$

(c) $1 - $ (b) $= \frac{74}{105}$

4 (a) $\frac{1}{36}$

(b) (i) $\left(\frac{5}{6}\right)^n$ (ii) $1 - \left(\frac{5}{6}\right)^n$

5 (a)   **Box A**   **Box B**

Box A:
20% — Red; 50% — Blue; 30% — Black
Box B (from Red): 50% — Red, 15% — Blue, 35% — Black
Box B (from Blue): 50% — Red, 15% — Blue, 35% — Black
Box B (from Black): 50% — Red, 15% — Blue, 35% — Black

(b) 10%   (c) 28%

Index

Orders: please contact Bookpoint Ltd, 130 Milton Park, Abingdon, Oxon OX14 4SB.
Telephone: (44) 01235 827720, Fax: (44) 01235 400454. Lines are open
9.00–5.00, Monday to Saturday, with a 24-hour message answering service.
Visit our website at www.hoddereducation.co.uk

© Howard Baxter, Mike Handbury, John Jeskins, Jean Matthews, Mark Patmore,
Brian Seager and Eddie Wilde 2004

First Published in 2004 by
Hodder Education, an Hachette UK Company
338 Euston Road
London NW1 3BH

Impression number   10 9 8 7 6 5
Year   2009

Cover photo © Comstock/Alarmy
Typeset by Pantek Arts Ltd
Printed in the UK by CPI Antony Rowe.

A catalogue record for this title is available from the British Library

ISBN: 978 0 340 81578 6